Wilmington – The Way We Lived

The first book I wrote about my life, *"Chinquapin-The Way We Lived,"* told the story of my life in and around Chinquapin until I was twelve years of age. This book is a continuation of my life story after my family moved to Wilmington in January, 1951.

I graduated from New Hanover High School in May, 1954 and worked for two and one-half years as a Manager Trainee for S. H. Kress & Co., in Wilmington and in Raleigh until I joined the U. S. Air Force in January, 1957.

I kept a diary in some of those years and it has proven to be of great benefit in recalling my experiences as a student at New Hanover High School and at S. H. Kress & Co.

I want to thank my sister, Sudie Goldston, and my two brothers, Gerald and Coleman, who have helped me recall some of the details of those experiences and events. Where there was some disagreement among us as to the details, I chose to go with my memories.

The photograph on the book cover is a shot of North Front Street in downtown Wilmington in the 1950's. If you look carefully, you can see the Bailey Theatre in the lower right corner of the photo and the S. H. Kress & Co. store just across the street. The photo brings back a lot of memories for me as I worked at both these businesses; at the Bailey while a NHHS student and at S. H. Kress after graduation.

CONTENTS

CONTENTS, continued

Chapter 1
From Chinquapin to Wilmington

The last you heard of me, I had just made friends with a wrestling gorilla, one that I and two of my fifth grade school friends had confronted on the stage at Chinquapin School. This momentous event in my life took place in September, 1948. Daddy told me this occasion would be a major turning point in my life, that I was destined for great things.

If you read my first book *"Chinquapin-The Way We Lived"*, you know that Daddy believed it was important that each of his children should have a totem like the Indian tradition. He got this tradition from his father - my Papa, J. B. Maready-who had made the lion the totem for Daddy. Daddy was born in July which has the zodiac sign of Leo. Because the midwife at my birth told Daddy that I looked like a little monkey, he had selected the gorilla as my totem.

After my triumph over the wrestling gorilla, I waited patiently for the next two years for something wonderful to happen, but it never did. But then in December, 1950, something happened that changed my life forever.

In the fall of 1950, Mother decided it would be better to leave Daddy. His drinking binges were happening more often and sometimes lasting a period of two or three weeks. The question was where should we move? Her first cousin, Nellie Meyland, who lived in Wilmington and worked in the office of an apartment complex, persuaded her Wilmington would be the best place.

There were still four children at home; Joan, age 16, me, age 14, Gerald, age 11, and Coleman, age 6. Our oldest brother, Jack, had joined the Navy at 17 in 1947 and was stationed on a mine sweeper in Charleston, South Carolina. Our oldest sister, Sudie, had graduated from Chinquapin High School in 1950 and was working as a telephone switchboard operator for Southern Bell in Jacksonville.

The decision to move was very difficult but the move itself seemed almost impossible. When to move, what to move, and getting someone with a truck to move our belongings required a lot of planning. Mother decided to move in December, 1950, after Christmas while school was out for the holidays.

What to move was fairly easily decided as we didn't have much furniture anyway; three beds, an old couch, three wooden chairs, a small dining room table with seven chairs, two chests of drawers, and two washstands constituted most of our furnishings that would be taken to Wilmington.

It was difficult to hire someone with a truck to help us move. Everyone in the Chinquapin area knew Daddy and was aware of his temper. Finally, two young brothers, Frank and Jessee James, were persuaded to help. They were sons of a highly respected bootlegger, Quinton James, and like their father, didn't mind taking a risk.

Mr. James was impartial to lawbreakers and decided to name his sons after two of the most notorious. They had felt a little embarrassed by their names in their younger years but were now somewhat proud of them.

They borrowed their father's truck and showed up early on Wednesday, December 27. We had packed our stuff on Tuesday and were ready to go when the James brothers drove up.

Fortunately, Daddy was on one of his worst drinking binges that Christmas. He spent two or three days after Christmas Day in the bedroom Gerald and I used, sleeping away. He wasn't sober enough to realize or care what was going on right under his nose. We didn't leave him a note. His family ran away from home.

Joan remained behind so as to finish the first school semester at Chinquapin School. She was in the tenth grade. Mid-term exams were given around the middle of January. She arranged to stay with her friend, Maxine Lanier, until the mid-term exams were over.

Frank, Mother and Coleman rode in the truck cab while Jessee, Gerald, and I rode in the back of the truck holding on to the furniture to keep it from falling off. Before we left, the James brothers told us they always stopped at Paul's Place for a hot dog whenever they were in the Rocky Point area. As we approached the intersection of Highways 117 and 133, Frank slowed down and pulled into the parking lot at Paul's Place.

He jumped out of the truck and asked "Have y'all ever had one of Paul's Place hot dogs? They's the best hot dogs in the world. Them at Billy Brinkley's in Chinquapin or at Elsie Maready's store in Mill Swamp ain't anywhere near as good. Me and Jessee always stop to get us one when we're delivering a load of Daddy's moonshine in this part of the country."[1]

I finished my hot dog before the others and walked outside to see if anything had fallen off the truck. As I was waiting, a man came out of the store with a large toothpick dangling from his lower lip. I could tell from his greasy clothing, smelling of gasoline, that he was probably an auto mechanic.

"Y'all moving?" He asked.

"Yes sir," I answered.

"Where from and where to?"

"We're moving from Chinquapin to Wilmington."

"Chinquapin? I've heard of a mechanic in Chinquapin. I cain't remember his first name but his last name is Moretti, or something like that. I think he's Italian. Do you know anybody like that?"

I didn't know what to say. I didn't want to tell somebody that knew Daddy where we were moving. We didn't want him to know.

"Maybe you mean the mechanic, Mr. Register, Orey Register, That sounds a little like Moretti", I said. "He has a garage right next to Billy Brinkley's store."

"That's probably it," he said. "The next time I'm in Chinquapin, I'll look him up." He climbed into his truck but couldn't get it started; a problem most mechanics seemed to have. A couple of men came out of Paul's Place, saw his trouble, and the three of us were able to give him a push until the engine caught. He roared off in a big cloud of smoke and headed towards Rocky Point.

After everyone was back in our truck, we headed for Wilmington. After crossing the Northeast Cape Fear River

---

[1] Paul's Place opened in 1928 at the intersection of Highways 117 and 133 in Pender County, and has been the place to get hot dogs since in that area of the state.

Bridge, we encountered a road block in the Castle Hayne area. Law enforcement officers were stopping vehicles in both lanes. While waiting for the vehicles ahead of us to move on, Jessee jumped out of the back of the truck and replaced Frank as the driver.

When the deputies approached our truck, one of them asked to see Jessee's driver's license. After studying it for a minute, he looked up and said, "So you're the famous Jesse James, huh? I don't suppose you stole this load of furniture, did you?" And he smiled to indicate he was only joking.

"By the way," he said. "I saw y'all change drivers while you were waiting to pull up. I need an explanation."

"Oh," Jessee answered. "That was my brother, Frank. He's been driving all the way from Chinquapin and just needed to take a break. While we were stopped, we thought it was a good time to change."

"So you have a brother named Frank?" The deputy asked. "Hey, Charlie, come over here and listen to this," he yelled out to another deputy. "We've got the James brothers trying to get through our road block. What do you think we ort to do with them?" He smiled again to show he was joking.

He then asked Frank to get out of the truck and present his driver's license as he suspected something wasn't right. He was right in his assessment of the situation. Frank didn't have a driver's license. It had been taken away months earlier when he was caught delivering a load of moonshine for his father.

The deputy wrote Frank a ticket for driving without a license. He didn't smile as he wrote the ticket. The court date was set for January 12, 1951, at the New Hanover County courthouse. Of course, Frank never showed up for the hearing.

I had mixed feelings about moving from Chinquapin to Wilmington. I understood we needed to separate ourselves from Daddy but I was enjoying myself at Chinquapin School. Although I was only in the ninth grade, I pictured myself as a BMOC. Not only had I wrestled a gorilla to a draw, which made me highly popular, I was the top student in the ninth grade except for Molly James. I had also been elected President of the freshman class.

I believed myself to be a great athlete and had recently won a spot on the boys' high school basketball team. I was one of the best tobacco "croppers" around and had saved the lives of three boys while swimming in the nearby Northeast Cape Fear River.[2]

I even had an impression, an erroneous one I later learned, that a lot of ninth grade girls wanted me to be their boyfriend.

We pulled in front of 3410 Adams Street, Riverside Apartments, around 1:30 P.M. As there were several of us working and as there wasn't much furniture, we had everything inside the apartment by 4:00 P.M. and the James brothers were on their way back to Chinquapin.

The apartment we moved into was a wonderful place. The amenities and conveniences were almost more than I could comprehend; things that only the most affluent people in Chinquapin enjoyed were available for our use and comfort.

There were overhead electric lights in every room that could be turned on and off with just the flip of a switch. In Chinquapin, we only had one electric light in the house. It was a sixty watt bulb on the end of a very long electric extension cord. It hung on a nail in the hallway where the kerosene space heater was located. If light was needed in other rooms, you could take the light off the nail and walk to the room where light was needed. However, that wasn't necessary very often as kerosene lamps were available in the bedrooms as well as in the kitchen.

In the apartment, there were electrical receptacles here and there into which a radio or lamps could be plugged. We did have a radio but it was battery powered and therefore the electrical receptacles were of little use to our family for some time before we could afford to purchase electric lamps. We had brought our kerosene lamps with us.

Mother was pleased to learn the stove was powered by electricity rather than by gas. Her stove in Chinquapin was a gas stove and she had endured several minor explosions while we lived there. Fortunately, she had never been injured seriously, just some singed eyebrows and hair.

---

[2] See my second Book *Chinquapin-All It's Cracked Up To Be*

To our delight, the apartment had a refrigerator. We never had one before. Mother could now buy fresh meat and not have to cook it on the day of purchase. Foodstuffs that had never been available to us before could now be put into the refrigerator without fear of spoiling. A wonderful benefit to having a refrigerator was that our Pepsi-Colas were kept cold so we didn't have to put ice into our glasses. We could drink our cold Pepsis right out of the bottle.

The indoor plumbing was even more wonderful than the electricity. Never in our wildest imagination would we have dreamed of having an inside commode or a bathtub. We had always had an outhouse and our baths were taken by use of a foot tub or a wash pan. Water had come from an outside hand pump.

The water at our Mill Swamp house had been very good but the water at our house in Chinquapin had a strong odor and taste of gasoline due to the disposal of dirty gas that Daddy used in cleaning automobile parts in his mechanic's work. As the hand pump was located just outside the garage door, it was the most convenient spot to dump dirty gas.

When we learned the City of Wilmington charged for the use of water, we did cut back on the number of baths. But Mother insisted the commode should be flushed each time it was used no matter the cost.

It was wonderful how the small coal-fired heater could heat the entire apartment, upstairs and downstairs. Neither of our two previous houses had any insulation. They both had cracks in the walls and floors, and with several broken window panes, the entire house was very cold in the winter with the exception of the kitchen in which the kerosene space heater was located. Whatever the temperature was outside, summer or winter, that was the temperature inside.

We had lived in Riverside two or three weeks when Mother decided to have a telephone installed; number RO-23310. I didn't know anyone in Wilmington who had a telephone but as we were on a two party line, I made use of it by listening to conversations of the other party. I had to make sure Mother didn't see me listening. I also had to keep Gerald and Coleman quiet.

Riverside Apartments was constructed during World War II to help provide affordable housing for the hundreds of families who moved to Wilmington to work in the shipyard. The North Carolina Shipbuilding Company, on the Cape Fear River, was within walking distance of Riverside Apartments. At one time, the company employed close to 20,000 civilian workers. Two hundred and forty-three ships were built there during the war.

There were approximately twenty red brick buildings with five apartments in each building. The buildings were located on both sides of Adams and Jefferson Streets from Southern Boulevard to Virginia Avenue. Each apartment had a kitchen, a living room with two bedrooms and a bathroom upstairs. When first built in 1943, the monthly rent was $37.50 for an interior apartment and $40.85 for a corner apartment.

When we moved to Riverside in December, 1950, the monthly rent was $45. The only source of income for our family of five at that time was a monthly allotment of $115 from the U. S. Navy my older brother, Jack, had applied for. The Navy took $60 out of his monthly pay of $100 and added $55 to make the total check $115. Out of that small sum,

Mother was able to pay the rent and utility bills, buy food and clothing and give the four children school lunch money. Needless to say, we didn't enjoy many luxuries.

Fortunately, after two or three months, Sudie was able to get a transfer from Jacksonville to the Wilmington Southern Bell office. She worked the evening shift in the downtown office, on Princess Street between Front and Second Streets, and rode the city bus to and from work. She was able to contribute several dollars each month to our income.

After she came to live with us there were six living in the two bedroom apartment; Mother, Joan, Gerald, Coleman, Sudie and me. At various times, our grandfather, Mother's father, would spend some time with us, making a total of seven living there. It was difficult to find the bathroom unoccupied anytime, day or night.

I thought Riverside was a wonderful place. In addition to all the amenities and conveniences I was enjoying, someone had put up a basketball goal behind one of the apartment buildings on Jefferson Street. There were several boys my age that lived in nearby apartments as well as several young Marines who lived there with their families. They commuted every day to Camp LeJeune to their military duties. We had a lot of fun playing basketball on that dusty, or muddy, court.

There was a small neighborhood grocery store, Dillon's Grocery, about four blocks away, at the corner of Jefferson Street and Southern Boulevard, where we bought all our groceries and household supplies. It seemed I had to go there almost every day for Mother.

It wasn't a long walk but I made it more difficult by trying to roller skate to the store. Coleman or Gerald had gotten a cheap pair of skates for Christmas. My thought was I could save a lot of time by skating rather than walking. I wasn't good at roller skating and the roller skates weren't the best. I had a lot of difficulty in keeping the skates on.

They just wouldn't stay adjusted to the length I needed. I had to stop every few feet, adjust them to the length of my feet, strap them back on and try again. The roller skate key seemed to be defective. The trip back with an armful of groceries was really painful. It would take me almost thirty minutes to get back home whereas if I had walked, it would have taken only twenty minutes.

There was a much larger grocery store at the corner of Carolina Beach Road and Southern Boulevard, Batson's Grocery. It was owned by the parents of one of my ninth grade classmates, Pleasant Batson, Junior. It was so much larger than Billy Brinkley's store or Van Bradham's store in Chinquapin I couldn't find my way around. I felt much more comfortable in Dillon's Grocery.

Teague's Barber Shop

Teague's Barber Shop was also within walking distance on Carolina Beach Road across from Legion Stadium. I enjoyed getting my haircuts there. Mr. Teague's scissors and clippers weren't as dull and didn't pull my hair as much as those of William Maready back in Mill Swamp. However, the price he charged for a haircut was considerably higher than the price charged by William. Gerald, Coleman and I let our hair grow much longer in Wilmington than we had in Chinquapin.

Mr. Teague was the father of one of my NHHS classmates, Billy Teague. It seemed a lot of my classmates' fathers had their own business.

Chapter 2
Getting Started at NHHS

In Chinquapin when someone began school or transferred from another school, they just had to show up and the principal and teachers would sort things out for them and get them in the right class. It wasn't that easy at NHHS. A lot of paperwork had to be completed. Mother wasn't up to the task. Neither were Joan, my 10th grade sister, or me. Fortunately, Mother's cousin, Nellie Meyland, had a son, Laverne, who was in the twelfth grade.

Laverne had a car and carried Joan and me to NHHS in the afternoon before our first day there. He took us into the office of the principal, Mr. Dale Spencer, introduced us and helped get us enrolled.

Instead of a school bus, a city bus, chartered from the Wilmington Transit Authority, rode through Riverside Apartments each morning to pick up students. It cost ten cents to ride the bus in the morning and ten cents again in the afternoon for the return trip. In addition to picking up students who lived in Riverside, the bus also rode through the nearby Sunset Park subdivision.

The houses in Sunset Park were very attractive with beautiful lawns and shrubbery. There was nothing in Chinquapin like them. No matter which street the bus went down, Washington, Adams, Jefferson, Monroe, Jackson, Van Buren, Harrison, Northern Boulevard, or Central Boulevard, the houses were so beautiful and the students waiting for the bus were so well-dressed, I thought everyone who lived there must be wealthy.

Later, as I found my way around, I learned several NHHS students lived in Riverside Apartments, and the nearby neighborhoods of Maffit Village and Sunset Park: Philip Morgan, Dickie Manning, Alice Evans, Grier White, Stanley Thompson, Ann Croom, Alice Dannenbaum, Billy Teague, Sammy Hill, and Douglas Morgan, to mention a few.

The first day Joan and I rode the bus to school, we were very nervous. I felt completely out of place and very anxious. The boy sitting next to me on the bus must have sensed my anxiety. "Hey," he said to me. "I don't think I've seen you before. My name's Sammy. What's yours?"

"Kenan", I answered. "Today's my first day going to school. We just moved here from Chinquapin".

"Kenan? I never heard of anybody with that name and I never heard of Chinquapin. I know there's a Kenan football stadium at Carolina and I think I've heard of a little town in Duplin County with the name of Kenansville. Did your family have anything to do with naming them?"

I was fairly sure no one in my family had anything to do with naming football stadiums or towns. "No", I replied. "I was just named after one of my great-uncles."

Just at that time, the bus had to stop at a traffic light while a fire truck, with its siren going full blast, sped through the intersection. Sammy jumped up, ran to the front of the bus, and watched the fire truck until it was out of sight. When he came back to our seat, he said to me, "I love fire trucks. I'd really like to ride on one someday. When I finish school, I'm gonna be a fireman."[3]

When we arrived at NHHS, Sammy walked inside with me and showed me where my homeroom was. "I'll see you later today after school. We'll sit together again. I'd like to know more about Chinquapin."

Sammy and I became good friends. He lived directly behind me at Riverside on Jefferson Street. On some afternoons, I would walk over to his apartment and visit. He had an incredible inventory of books and games. Sometimes,

---

[3] Sam Hill was appointed Fire Chief for the City of Wilmington in 1988.

we walked over to the outdoor basketball court in the next block and played basketball.

I really felt out of place at NHHS. I was just a scared country boy trying to find his way around a very large city school. I learned quickly no other boys wore jeans to school, or overall pants as we called them in Chinquapin. Brogans were another item that no one wore to school. Those two articles were staples of my clothing wardrobe. Despite our tight budget, I convinced Mother I had to have some city school clothes.

She and I rode the bus the next Saturday downtown to the Sears, Roebuck Store on North Front Street. This was our first visit to a Sears' store. We could look around and buy exactly what I needed, as long as the price was low enough. Our prior experiences with Sears was ordering something from their catalog and then getting a letter saying "We are temporarily out of stock of the items you ordered. We trust the substituted items will be satisfactory." They never were satisfactory.

On my first day at NHHS, I was taken to an English class, taught by Mr. Daniel Todd. The class was in process when I was brought in and introduced to the class. I thought I detected some smirks and suppressed giggles when it was announced I was transferring from Chinquapin High School. That didn't help my confidence very much.

After I was seated and the class had returned to its struggle with dangling participles, the boy sitting in the row next to me, leaned over and, in a whisper, introduced himself. "My name's Sammy Ranzino," he said. I was startled to learn he had the same name as the star basketball player for North Carolina State University.

He then grinned and whispered "I'm not really Sammy Ranzino. My name's Vernon. I moved here from Wallace a couple of years ago. After our class is over, I want to talk to you some more." That is how I first met Vernon Meshaw, my closest friend at NHHS and for years afterwards.

After English class was over, my next class was World History. Vernon showed me the classroom where that course was taught. The teacher was Miss Reba Russ, a short, little woman, who put up with no nonsense, a trait that I leaned the great majority of NHHS teachers possessed.

Miss Russ assigned me to a seat just ahead of a beautiful girl. Her name was Jane Love. Jane introduced herself and welcomed me to the class. She was smart, she was friendly, and she was very pretty. It made me feel better for someone like her to make friends with me.

The history class was made up of sophomores. I was the only freshman in the class. All the students, including Jane, were a year ahead of me. The difference in our ages made me feel a little more insecure.

After World History, I had a math class, taught by Ms. Sanders. My seat was in front of David Melvin. David and I later became friends, but on that first day, he felt it was necessary to teach someone, with a name like Kenan from a place named Chinquapin, a thing or two about city schools.

He pulled my hair, punched me in the back, and jolted my desk, feeling that a young boy from the country would be too intimidated to hit back. He even made a derogatory comment about my overall pants and my brogans.

I put up with this treatment for a while, but when Ms. Sanders was called out into the hall to speak to someone from the office, I reached back, grabbed David's pencil, broke it in half, and threw the two pieces at him. He drew back into his seat, not expecting this kind of reaction.

"What'd you do that for"? He asked. "I was just trying to make friends. You owe me for my pencil."

"Put that on my bill", I replied. "And I'll settle up with you after school lets out."

Just then Ms. Sanders came back into the room. David and I were both pouring over our textbook when she looked around the room. "I thought I heard talking", she said. "Who was talking while I was out?"

David spoke up. "Me and Kenan were talking. I dropped my pencil under his desk and I asked him to get it for me. And he did. That's all."

She eyed us suspiciously but decided to accept his explanation. She turned to the blackboard and finished writing the problem about when did Train A overtake Train B if it left thirty minutes later and was going fifty miles an hour while Train B was going forty miles an hour.

Vernon had arranged to meet at lunch near the bicycle rack. He brought with him a close friend, Leonard Williams, and we were introduced. Both Vernon and Leonard advised me to never eat in the lunch room. You could get a cold lunch or a hot lunch but, according to them, both were awful.

Instead, they took me across 13th street to a little café with the name, "Pete's Place". The place was packed full of students and I didn't think we would ever be able to place our order. But Pete had devised an efficient plan that allowed him to serve his customers rapidly. He and his staff had made sandwiches and hot dogs earlier that morning and all he had to do was to grab out of a warmer whatever the student wanted.

The most popular item seemed to be a hot dog, which is what Vernon recommended to me. When I got it, it was loaded down with chili, neither the bun nor the hot dog was hot, and the bun was soggy with all that chili. Regardless, everyone seemed to enjoy Pete's hot dogs. If Billy Brinkley had tried to serve hot dogs like that in Chinquapin, his customers would have started patronizing Sam Bostic's store.

After lunch, we walked to the front of the school where we talked until it was time to go to our next class. My class was on the second floor and I started to walk up the large steps in the middle of the school. Vernon quickly grabbed me and told me to never walk up or down those steps. They were reserved for use by seniors only. If I was caught using those steps by some seniors, I could be killed or worse.

My first day at NHHS hadn't been too bad. I had made four friends, Sammy Hill, Vernon Meshaw, Leonard Williams, Jane Love and one potential enemy, David Melvin. I had learned not to ever use the Senior Steps or eat in the lunchroom. I had learned all about the food in Pete's Place, but I wondered if the lunch room meals could be any worse than Pete's hot dogs.

Gradually, I began to feel more comfortable at NHHS. I made a few friends in Riverside; made some more on the bus rides to and from school, and made a few more in some of my classes.

Basketball season was underway and as I was an avid basketball fan, I asked Vernon and Leonard to go with me to the next NHHS basketball game. They wanted to go also and we agreed to meet outside the high school gym on Princess Street at 5:30 PM on the night of the game. We met at the appointed time, bought our tickets, and went inside to the balcony seating.

I had never seen such a magnificent arena. It was so much better than the old gym at Chinquapin. Even the gym at Wallace High School couldn't compare. The stands were full of people. The balcony seats were filled mostly by NHHS students who kept up a continuous roar in response to the energetic cheerleaders with their amazing cheers and acrobatics.

We were playing the team from Needham Broughton High School in Raleigh, who I quickly learned was our arch rival. The Junior Varsity game was in progress when we entered. The game was very close but NHHS won by a narrow margin.

The star of the JV team didn't look much like a star player. He had red hair and was a little pudgy in my opinion. But he ran the team well and seemed to be able to score at will. Vernon told me his name was Sonny Jurgensen and big things were expected from him next year, especially on the football field. I had my doubts. I took a wait and see attitude.

When the JV game was over and the varsity team ran out on the floor, the crowd stood up and roared its support. Leonard said, "We've got a really good team this year. Everybody's expecting us to win the state championship."

"Who's that man with the team that looks like an undertaker?" I asked him. "What's he doing out there? Everybody's gathered all around him. Is he going to have a prayer?"

"Are you crazy"? Leonard asked. "That's their coach, Coach Leon Brogdon, the best high school coach in the state". I had my doubts about their coach. I decided to take another wait and see attitude.

Chapter 3
Sunset Park Roller Skating Rink

Leonard and I made plans one Saturday afternoon to go to the Sunset Roller Skating Rink on Shipyard Boulevard. He rode his bike from his home at Nesbitt Courts to my home in

Riverside Apartments on Adams Street. He had planned to be there by two p.m. but hadn't arrived at 3 o'clock. I had about given him up when he came up sweating profusely. I could tell he had been walking the pedals for some time.

"What happened? Where've you been?" I asked. "You're about an hour late. I thought you weren't coming,"

"Well, first off, Ma made me clean up my room before she'd let me leave," he panted. "You've seen my room. How long do you think it'd take you to clean up a room like that? And then, on the way over, I decided to take Burnett Boulevard rather than Carolina Beach Road. That was a big mistake. You cain't believe all the big trucks coming and going on Burnett to the State Ports. Every truck driver that passed me blew his horn for me to get off the road. I thought I was going to die. I finally decided to turn on Northern Boulevard and go over to Carolina Beach Road,"

"Well, that couldn't have made you an hour late," I complained. "What else happened?"

"When I turned into Southern Boulevard, Pleasant Batson was emptying some trash from their grocery store. He saw me and called me over. You know I've been trying to get a job at a grocery store. He knew that and told me I ort to go in and talk to his Daddy right then. One of their stock boys had just quit. I knew I was gonna be late but I had to go in and talk to Mr. Batson. I can tell you that Batson's Grocery Store is one busy place. Everybody in Sunset Park, Riverside Apartments and Maffit Village shop there, according to Pleasant,"

"Well, did you get a job?" I asked him.

"Naah, he didn't want a friend of Pleasant to be working with him. He thought there'd be more talking and fooling around than working. I didn't think that should have cost me getting the job but what could I do," he said. "I hopped back on my bike and got here as quick as I could. You ready to go?"

As I didn't have a bike, Leonard left his beside the steps to our apartment and we walked down Adams Street to Shipyard Boulevard and then over to the skating rink. Not wanting to have to rent a pair of skates, I took my old pair, the ones that gave me a lot of trouble on my skating trips to Dillon's

Grocery to buy groceries. My hope was the skates would perform better on a smooth skating rink floor.

There were a lot of bicycles and cars in the parking lot. It looked as if everybody wanted to get in some skating that afternoon. It was fairly cold and windy so that skating indoors was much better than trying to do something outside.

When we walked through the door, a blast of noise greeted us. Boys and girls were shouting or singing, small children were crying, mamas were trying to get their smaller children to behave, and the rink had its roller skating music turned up full blast.

Leonard went over to the desk to rent a pair of skates while I put mine on. As usual, I had trouble getting my left skate tight enough to stay put. The tightening apparatus would slip sometimes without prevarication.

We started skating side by side but Leonard soon left me in the dust. He was a good skater while the only skating I had ever done was on the small patch of cement in front of the Chinquapin post office and to Dillon's Grocery after we moved to Wilmington.

A lot of skaters whizzed by me as I tried to maintain my balance. I had been attending New Hanover High School just a few weeks and knew only a few students. I wasn't sure but I thought I recognized a few of them as they went by; Bubba Pursley, Derris Bradshaw, Millard Williams, Ralph Christmas, Hawk Saunders, Willard Jordan, etc. They all lived in the Maffit Village area, just across Shipyard Boulevard from the skating rink. As they passed me, I didn't get a good look as I was concentrating on keeping my balance and my skates on.

We had been there just a few minutes when a group of rowdy boys came in. Leonard pulled to a stop by me as I was hanging on the rail to keep from falling. "Look," he said. "There's Charlie Niven and some of the football team. His nickname's Barrell. He's probably the best high school football player in the state. I heard he's been offered a football scholarship at Duke. I bet he's good at skating like he is in every other sport,"

"Why is he called Barrell?" I asked. "I see he's kinda short and stocky but he's a long way from looking like a barrel,"

Leonard answered. "Well, I never thought about it. I don't know. If I get a chance today, I think I might just ask him about that nickname."

Charlie and his teammates went over to the desk, got their skates, and within a few minutes were out on the floor, dominating the rink. In tribute to Charlie "Barrell" Niven, the rink attendant played *"Roll Out the Barrell"* on the PA system. Charlie was soon performing a lot of skating moves that were done by professional skaters.

Most of the other skaters pulled to the side to watch him perform. I had almost reached the railing when my left skate came off. I bent down to put it back on just as Charlie was showing off his ability to skate backwards. He didn't see me as he came zooming along and hit me broadsides. He did a flip and landed on his head. He lay there for a few moments while everyone ran to his side asking him if he was okay.

"Are you okay, Charlie? Can you stand up, Barrell?" He was a little groggy but soon stood up to the cheers of the crowd.

My nose was bleeding some, where one of his skates had struck, but no one noticed. Charlie came over to me and let me have a piece of his mind, what little he had left after the crash. "What's wrong with you? Didn't you see me coming? Why don't you get some good skates, you cheap skate? If you cain't keep your skates on, you ort not to be out here anyway." He said a few other choice words I was surprised to hear from such a celebrity but his teammates were not taken aback. They may have been accustomed Barrell's cussing.

I took off my other skate, went to the side and sat down. Barrell resumed his skating performance to the delight of the spectators.

His group left at the same time as Leonard and I did. Leonard decided it would be a good time to ask about his nickname.

Charlie wasn't bothered by Leonard's question. He seemed to be proud of his nickname. "Well, to tell the truth, I never was quiet about how good I was at sports. One of my coaches in Junior High told me my head was so big a barrel wouldn't hold it. Some friends started calling me "barrelhead". They shortened it to "Barrell" later and that's what happened."

"Say, what about your little friend there?" as he pointed at me. "I could've had a bad injury. I could've lost my football scholarship to Duke."

"He's really sorry about what happened," Leonard answered. "He's from Chinquapin and this was his first trip to a skating rink. He don't know much about anything except cropping tobacco. I told him he should've rented a pair of skates but he's too cheap for that. Maybe next time he'll listen to me."

"Thanks for sticking up for me," I said to Leonard as Charlie and his friends drove off. "You could've told him I was an A student."

"Yeah, that would've really impressed him. From what I hear, he don't care a lot about grades and stuff like that," Leonard told me.

I decided that day the Sunset Park Roller Skating Rink was too dangerous for me; I would stick just to skating to Dillon's Grocery.

School was out in late May and I felt I hadn't done too badly at NHHS my first year. I had made good grades, despite being a transfer from a small country school, and had made some good friends.

Other than getting off to a bad start with my overall pants, my brogans, and saying "I swanee" on occasions, I hadn't embarrassed myself too much.

Chapter 4
My Sister Saves Us

When we first moved to Wilmington, Mother believed we could get by, financially speaking, on the military allotment Jack provided for us. She learned quickly it cost more to live in Wilmington than it did in Chinquapin. She didn't want to but she finally contacted Sudie and asked if she could transfer to Wilmington and help us out.

Sudie was a very intelligent, hard-working, young lady and if she had been born in any other family, would have probably gone off to college. Our family had no extra money to pay for college tuition, room and board, so she was relegated to finding employment wherever she could. One of her high school teachers had helped her apply for a college scholarship at several small colleges without any expectation of getting one.

But one day to her surprise and elation, while she was still working behind the lunch counter at Billy Brinkley's store, she received a letter from Davis & Elkins College, a small liberal arts college in Elkins, West Virginia, informing her they were awarding her a scholarship. She spent the next few days telling all her friends and her former school teachers about her good fortune. She pictured herself, with a liberal arts degree, coming back to Chinquapin High School in four years and teaching those unlearned Chinquapin youngsters a thing or two about English, or perhaps history, or even civics.

There were several long discussions among Sudie, Mother and Daddy as to how she was to get to Elkins in August, 1950, before classes began. Elkins was some 450 miles away from Chinquapin. No one in our family had ever traveled that far before. Overnight trips were unheard of.

Fortunately, for the first time in our family, Daddy had a good car to drive. It really wasn't his but was owned by Jack. He had been in the Navy for almost three years, had saved some money, and was getting Navy wages of around $100 per month. He decided to buy a nice car although he wasn't allowed to keep one at his naval base in Charleston. However, it would be there for him to drive when he came home on leave.

On one of his weekend leaves, he and Daddy went to Wallace to Cavenaugh's Auto Sales where he purchased an almost new 1948 four door Ford sedan. No longer did we have to push Daddy to get his car started. The Ford started every time. It was clean and shiny when Jack brought it home and he was reluctant to let his siblings get into the car. But as it turned out, it wasn't his siblings he should have been worried about, it was Daddy. As an auto mechanic, his clothing was almost always greasy and reeking of oil and gasoline. It wasn't long before Jack's new car had lost that new car look and smell.

It was decided Mother and Daddy would take Sudie to Elkins in Jack's car. She could have gone by Greyhound but Daddy wanted to take a long trip in Jack's new car while it still ran. They would make it a vacation trip, something they had heard other people talk about. Daddy heard other men talk about how fast they could drive from Town A to Town B. This trip would give him a chance to beat the record of other drivers in Chinquapin, especially Rock Bradham, who loved to brag about his driving skills.

As Coleman was too young to be left in the care of Joan, Gerald, or me, it was decided to take him along on the fun trip. For some reason, he and Sudie were unusually thirsty on the way to Elkins, but Daddy hated stopping as it would reduce his average rate of speed.

If Sudie or Mother spied a store along the highway and pointed it out to Daddy, he would say "I ain't going to stop at that d____ store. It don't look right to me. We'll see a better one up the road." They never did.

Daddy's plan was to drive all the way to Elkins, drop Sudie off at the college, spend one night near there and drive back home the next day. Enough baloney sandwiches were prepared to last them the entire trip and they could buy some Pepsi-Colas to drink when they had to stop for gasoline

They left very early in the morning and despite getting lost once or twice, they made it to the college just before dark. Sudie was dropped off at the administration building and Mother and Daddy sped off to drive a few miles on the way back to Chinquapin before dark. They made it as far as Beverly where they found a place that rented small cabins for as little as $3 a night. The accommodations, with inside plumbing and electricity, were much better than they were used to. But it did put a severe strain on their travel budget.

The next evening while several of the men were sitting around and discussing world affairs in Mr. Van Bradham's store, Daddy slyly brought up the subject of average rate of speed on long auto trips.

"Say, Rock," he asked Mr. Bradham's son, "tell us again about your driving to Richmond last year and how much time it took to go there and back."

Rock was always glad to brag about that trip. "Well, Lee, since you ask, it's about 230 miles to Richmond and 230 miles back. My old "48 Chevrolet Fleetmaster took me there and back in a little over nine hours driving time. That's about fifty miles a hour. I ain't heard of many men that can beat that. I know I don't ever want to drive that far and that fast again. It ain't safe."

Daddy casually replied, "That's pretty good, almost as good as what I just did. Me and Corinne took Sudie to Elkins, West Virginia, in my "48 Ford. It's 900 mile there and back and my driving time was just a little shy of 17 hours. I figure that to be almost fifty-three miles a hour. I didn't keep up with how much gas it took."

The other men began congratulating Daddy on such a driving accomplishment. They were really impressed. Poor Rock just sat there; his record driving time, of which he was so proud, was no longer anything he could brag about.

Mother and Daddy had only been home two days when Mr. Van Bradham sent someone over, late one afternoon, to tell them Mother had a telephone call from Sudie. This news scared her to death; she had never had a telephone call before. Mr. Bradham showed her how to hold the phone.

She held the phone close to her mouth and said "Hey, is that you, Sudie?"

Sudie explained she was in Wallace. She had caught the Greyhound from Elkins to Wallace. She was very distraught. She learned from her college counselor the morning after being dropped off at the Administration Building at Davis & Elkins her scholarship only paid for tuition, not for books, room and board and any other incidental expenses.

No one had bothered to tell her that before that long, expensive trip. Mother and Daddy didn't know enough about scholarships to ask any questions about Sudie's good fortune. She had stuck it out for a day or two, hoping something would work out, but it didn't.

Luckily, Sudie had saved a few dollars from her job at Billy Brinkley's store and had used most of that to purchase the bus ticket. She asked Mother to have Daddy drive to Wallace and bring her home; her college experience hadn't been all it was cracked up to be. Daddy grudgingly agreed to her request. "If she's got this far, she ort to be able to get to Chinquapin on her own. I'm always having to do something for our young'uns that take me away from my work."

When Sudie walked into Billy Brinkley's the next morning, everyone was surprised to see her: Billy, Margaret, Susie Sandlin and some of the regulars. She had to tell the whole embarrassing story but she decided it would be better to get it behind her and get on with her life. Billy happily agreed to let her return to work at the lunch counter.

However, Sudie's experience with placing the call to Mr. Van Bradham's store from Wallace made her aware of a career opportunity. While waiting for Mother to walk over to Mr. Bradham's telephone, she and the telephone operator had a friendly conversation about the glamorous lives of telephone operators. In the next few days, she did some checking and learned Southern Bell would train young ladies to become switchboard operators at no cost and would hire them after training.

She and a very distant cousin, who oddly enough had the same name, Sudie Jayne Maready, applied to Southern Bell and they were sent to Morehead City for training. The training took a few weeks and after she had mastered the skill necessary for a switchboard operator, she was transferred to the Southern Bell center in Jacksonville. She had worked there a few months when the call for help came from Mother. We needed her to move to Wilmington to supplement our income.

She agreed and within a few days had arranged for a transfer to the Wilmington office. Her feeling of independence was gone; in Jacksonville, she rented a room and was free to go and come as she pleased. Now she had to put up with Mother's demands as well as those of her sister and three brothers. From sleeping in a bed of her own, she now had to share a bed with others. She never knew who she would find in her bed when she came home. Her family didn't seem to appreciate her sacrifices.

Even though it was her money that bought us our Pepsi-Colas, etc., she hardly ever found an unopened one when she returned home after the evening shift. Gerald would even put a note on his half-full Pepsi that read "Don't anyone drink this and that means you, Sudie." Apparently, he believed she had taken a sip from his Pepsi on previous occasions.

In just a few short months, Sudie had gone from a scholarship winner with dreams of being a school teacher to a telephone switchboard operator without a bed to call her own. In accord with Robert Burns's famous poem "The best laid plans of mice and men often go awry."

Chapter 5
We Move to Winter Park

As soon as school was over for the year, Mother told us she had made arrangements to rent a house in the Winter Park community, at the corner of Kerr and Wrightsville Avenues, across the street from Winter Park Presbyterian Church. The move was necessary she said because there just wasn't enough room in that tiny two bedroom apartment.

She then told us she had agreed to let Daddy come back to our family. He had promised her he would quit drinking, would get a job, and wanted to live with his wife and children very much. With Daddy back in our family, there were seven of us living together. The Riverside apartment just wouldn't accommodate such a large family.

Our new house was like a palace to me. It had a large, beautiful yard with large sycamore trees. There was a living room, a kitchen, a dining room and four bedrooms. It also had closets. We had never had closets before. Like Riverside Apartments, it had inside plumbing and electricity.

The rent was $60 a month which stretched Mother's budget to the limit even with Daddy's earnings available. She decided to try to rent one of the upstairs bedrooms. She quickly got a response to her newspaper ad from a Marine, Hoagy, and his wife, Betty. They had a baby boy, Hoagy, Jr., who had flaming red hair like his father.

Hoagy was stationed at Camp LeJeune and hitchhiked each day from Wilmington to Camp LeJeune and back. As there were several Marines living in the Wilmington area that drove back and forth to Camp LeJeune every day, getting a ride wasn't difficult. Betty stayed home all day and played cards with Joan. When Hoagy came back from Camp LeJeune at night he would do uniform alterations for some of his Marine buddies. He was quite good at it too. He would cut and snip and sew quietly with a Lucky Strike cigarette dangling from his lips.

With the addition of Hoagy and his family, there were now ten people living in the house.

I enjoyed living at Winter Park. There were a lot of boys about my age living in the area; Jimmy DeHart, Lewis Wallace, Larry Crawley, and Ken Newland among others. Also, a family from Cypress Creek, a small community near Chinquapin, moved into a house on Kerr Avenue, about a block from our house. Mother and Daddy knew Almon and Rubena James well and we knew their children; Eloise, Tink, Harrell and R. C. It was good to have someone living near you that you had known most of your life.

The Winter Park area wasn't heavily developed then. College Road didn't exist. Kerr Avenue, or Forty-Fifth Street, was the main roadway leading north. It ran all the way to Wrightsboro where it intersected with Highway 117. Forty-Sixth Street (now College Road) ended at Cedar Avenue in the northerly direction and at Shipyard Boulevard in a southerly direction. There was no direct road from Winter Park to Monkey Junction.

On the southwest corner of the intersection of Oleander Drive and Forty-Sixth Street, Mrs. Nellie Farrar lived. She maintained a herd of ponies in a pasture behind her house. The pasture was located where Vision Works, Verizon and Toys R Us are located today.

Hugh MacRae Park was within easy walking distance and that is where the neighborhood boys usually gathered to socialize. There was another attraction within walking distance, the Park-Vue Drive-in Theater. It was located near the intersection of Oleander Drive and Floral Parkway where Office Depot and Books-A-Million are now located.

None of the neighborhood boys had a car but we would walk over and stand outside the theater where we had a good view of the screen. We were at some disadvantage in that we had no idea what the actors and actresses were saying but we could use our imagination to ad lib for them. *Joan of Arc*, starring Ingrid Bergman, required some imaginative ad-libbing. I was the best ad-libber, and came up with some good ones as Ingrid was burning at the stake.

There was a small restaurant at 4612 Oleander Drive, Rollins Barbecue, which served some great barbecue. Local people declared its barbecue was as good, or better, than that at Skinner & Daniel's out on Market Street.

Chapter 6
Migrant Worker

I didn't have much time to enjoy living in Winter Park before I went back to Chinquapin that summer to earn some money by cropping tobacco. Due to our meager income, all of us were aware if there was any way to earn money, we had to take advantage of the opportunity. The only skill I had at the time was cropping tobacco. I was too young to get a worker's permit and probably wouldn't have been able to find a job in Wilmington anyway.

Mother had been in touch with a farmer that lived in the Mill Swamp area, someone she had known for many years. Riley Dail needed someone to stay with him that summer and help him put in tobacco. Gerald also was able to get a job that summer working in tobacco for the father of his best friend in Chinquapin.

So one day, early in July, 1951, Daddy took Gerald to the farm of Mr. Albert Sanderson, who lived about half-way between Chinquapin and Wallace, and took me to the home of Riley Dail.

Riley Dail and his wife, Eveline, had one child, Jerry, who was ten years old. Eveline, daughter of George and Epsy Maready, had a brother, Hilton, who also needed someone to help him put in tobacco. Between Riley and Hilton and another one of their relatives, they had enough tobacco to require five days of puttin' in each week.

Tobacco farmers preferred to have four croppers in the tobacco field. In addition to me, Riley hired the young brother of Hilton's wife, whose name was Phillip McClung, and two African-American brothers, Birdell and Johnny Hudson.

Birdell and Johnny were the sons of a well-respected widow in Mill Swamp, Ada Hudson. Birdell was a sophomore at N. C. Central University at the time but had come home for the summer to earn some money. Johnny was about my age as was Phillip.

So there we were working together every week day for about seven weeks, two young white boys and two young black boys. We got along very well except Phillip, who liked to sing, and forgetting who was in the field with him, would occasionally break out into a song, acapella, that had some words that were offensive to the feelings of blacks.

Birdell, who was five or six years older than we were, would take umbrage at the words in Phillip's songs and threaten him, in some well-chosen words, with bodily harm if he ever heard those words again. Phillip could go for several days without repeating his offense but invariably he would forget where he was and break out into another song. I feared that Birdell would one day break Phillip's head but all he ever did was threaten to do so.

At dinner time, Birdell, Johnny, and some black ladies who worked at the barn, had to wait while the white workers ate their meal. The blacks would then eat at the "second table,"

Gerald and I were migrant workers. We traveled from Wilmington, stayed with a family for several weeks, and did farm work for those families while we were there. After the season was over, we would migrate back to Wilmington.

Working all day from seven in the morning until six wasn't too bad but the evenings were very dull. There wasn't much to do in Mill Swamp, especially in the home of Riley Dail. I had no way of travel, not even a bicycle. Of course, there was no television. Riley and Evelina had an old battery powered radio but they could only get four stations: WSM in Nashville, WCKY in Cincinnati, WRRZ in Clinton and WPTF in Raleigh. They didn't like to listen to the programs I enjoyed.

I enjoyed listening to the Grand Old Opry on Saturday nights and to WCKY on week nights to their country music but Evelina didn't enjoy country music. She preferred to listen to "*Inner Sanctum*" and "*Yours Truly, Johnny Dollar,*" and such. There wasn't much for me to do but go to bed. I would get up early, eat breakfast, go out to the stable and hitch up the mule to the tobacco drag or to the cart if a barn of tobacco had to be taken out that morning.

The only break in this routine occurred on Saturdays. Generally, we didn't have to work in tobacco on that day. I would get up late, put on my Saturday clothes, and head for Chinquapin. It was about a three mile walk but usually somebody would come by who recognized me and would offer me a ride.

I went directly to Billy Brinkley's store and ordered two hot dogs with mustard and ketchup with a Pepsi-Cola for my Saturday lunch. After eating and talking with Margaret Ann, Billy's daughter, I'd walk into the pool room. Unless something really unusual was going on, there would be several local boys there: Raymond Earl Cottle, David Bradham, Jaycee Williams, Donald Lanier, O. J. Register, Freddy Futreal, Jeff Futreal, etc.

Pool wasn't my game so I just sat around and watched and listened to their enlightened conversation and sometimes offered my own opinion or told about how life was so different in Wilmington.

Sometime in the middle of the afternoon, most of us would walk to the swimming hole at the bridge over the Northeast Cape Fear River. We enjoyed ourselves there for two or three hours, playing water tag, getting bottom, or perhaps jumping off the bridge, feet first, or diving off the "Rock,"

The "Rock," on the east side of the river, was a rocky ledge some four or feet high. It was the only rock that could be found anywhere near Chinquapin. It had stains on it that resembled blood stains. For generations, the story had been passed down a skirmish had taken place on the ledge during the War Between the States and some soldiers had died there. It was exciting to think something like that had happened right there at our swimming hole.

Chinquapin Post Office

After we were tired out from swimming, we would walk back to Billy Brinkley's. For supper, I would order a Spam sandwich and a Pepsi-Cola. Then back into the pool room for some more socializing until dark.

Billy's was the favorite spot for teen-agers to hang out. There was a TV set on one of the shelves in the general merchandise section of the store. It was too bad the reception wasn't good enough to really see what show was on.

There was a juke box with all the latest country and popular hit songs. Some of the teen-agers prided themselves on being good dancers and provided some entertainment. Of course, I never danced but sometimes I found I was tapping my foot to such songs as "*On Top of Old Smoky*" by The Weavers. If I saw anyone watching, I quit immediately.

When night came, I would walk up the road to the Hula Drive-in Theatre, pay my ten cents admission and take a seat in the Chicken House. When Tom Sanderson had built the

Hula, he had foreseen people within walking distance might prefer to walk in rather than drive in, so a small building was put up right in front of the big screen to accommodate the walk-in people. It had a few rows of wooden benches to sit on and a glass window to view the movie. It came to be called the "Chicken House" as it somewhat resembled a large chicken house.

At this age, I was beginning to think about girls and there were usually a few I knew who were watching the movie in the Chicken House. Sometimes I would sit with one of them on the back row where we might hold hands and, if nobody was watching, sneak a quick kiss.

After the movie, I was faced with the problem with getting back to Riley Dail's. There weren't very many cars or trucks heading towards Mill Swamp at that time of night. Sometimes I would have to walk all the way back by myself. It would take me about an hour to get home.

One night, a friend of mine, Orren Cavenaugh, who lived in the Pin Hook area, offered me a ride as far as Mr. Emp Whaley's store. From there, it was only a mile to Riley Dail's. I thought Orren could have been accommodating and taken me all the way home but he didn't offer and I was reluctant to ask him.

When I got out of his pick-up at Mr. Emp's store and started walking, I recalled a prisoner who had been working on a road gang in that area had escaped the day before and was still on the loose. I became very frightened; every time I heard a noise from the bushes and trees alongside the road, I expected the convict to jump out and kill me. I would tell myself it was only a raccoon or a possum but sometimes I didn't believe what I told myself.

I ran as fast as I could the last few hundred yards and was completely out of breath when I burst into the living room where the Dails were listening to "*The Life of Reilly,*"

"What in the world's chasing you?" Evelina asked. "You look like you seen a ghost."

I was kind of embarrassed to tell them I had been running because I was afraid of being killed by an escaped convict. "Well, you needn't have been scared of that," Riley said. "He was captured early this morning. "Didn't anybody tell you that in Chinquapin?"

"No, nobody said anything about it. I think I'll go on to bed, if you don't mind and get up tomorrow morning and go to Sunday School. I ain't been since I've been here. Is tomorrow morning the Sunday that it's Preacher Garvin's turn to preach at our church? If it is, I think I'll stay for church too."

I was paid five dollars a day that summer and when tobacco season was over, I had saved almost $150. Mother was so happy to hear that when I went back home. I could give her $100 and use the other $50 to buy my school clothes for my sophomore year. I decided to shop for my school clothes at J. C. Penney at 243 North Front Street this time rather than at Sears, Roebuck. I liked the sales clerks better at Penney's.

Although I had made what seemed like a lot of money at the time, I decided farming wasn't for me. Tobacco farming was one of the dirtiest, most physically exhausting, careers that anyone could choose. I thought I could do better than that. I was determined to find some job in Wilmington so that I wouldn't have to return to Chinquapin in the summer of 1953.

Chapter 7
My Family Runs Away From Home

About two weeks before school started, my two aunts, Tish Hoffman and Adele Maready drove down from New Jersey to pay us a visit. They were sisters of Daddy. Aunt Tish had received her nursing training at James Walker Memorial Hospital but had moved to New Jersey to pursue her nursing career. Aunt Adele was a graduate of East Carolina Teachers College, had served in the U.S. WAVES during World War II and moved in with Aunt Tish after the war.

Aunt Tish had two young children, Bryant, age twelve and Jane, age seven. With the four of them, Mother had to find places for thirteen people to sleep. There would have been fourteen but Sudie had decided to get married while I was at Chinquapin during the summer. She and her fiancé went to

South Carolina to get married and then had moved in with his mother and brothers in a little house near the mountains at Trap Hill, North Carolina.

As our renters, Hoagy and Betty and their baby, were paying rent for the exclusive use their bedroom, Mother felt she couldn't ask them if they would allow her to put a pallet on their bedroom floor for two or three of her guests.

She was faced with the difficult task of finding a place for ten people to sleep in three bedrooms. She did it the old fashioned way. Pallets were made in the bedrooms, living room, and wherever there was empty floor space. Finally, everyone found a place to lay their heads.

Our New Jersey visitors had only been there a few minutes when Gerald, Bryant, Coleman and I decided to enjoy a football game. Bryant, who was somewhat large for his age, fell on Coleman while Coleman was making a dash for the end zone. In the encounter, Coleman's right arm was broken. Aunt Tish, Mother, Coleman and one or two others took off for the emergency room at James Walker Hospital. Coleman's arm was put in a cast but he wasn't able to resume our football game when they returned from the hospital. Their visit hadn't started well.

When it was time for Aunt Tish and Aunt Adele to return to New Jersey, they asked Mother if I could go back with them for a week's visit. Mother reluctantly agreed after they assured her it would be very easy for me to ride back to Wilmington on the Greyhound bus. They promised to pay my bus fare.

Early one Saturday morning, the five of us packed into Aunt Tish's car and headed to New Jersey. Mother and her family stood in the yard and waved goodbye with the exception of Coleman whose right arm was in a sling.

We made good time and arrived at a little town in Virginia very close to the Marine Base at Quantico. Aunt Adele had a marine friend there she had met while serving in the WAVES in Washington during World War II. He was now stationed at Quantico and Aunt Tish agreed to spend the night in a motel on Highway 1 so Adele and Charles could see each other.

Charles took us on a tour of the base, including a visit to the Quantico museum. The exhibits there showed the history of the Marines all the way back to 1804 when the Marines defeated the Barbary pirates at Tripoli. Many of the exhibits were about more recent battles in the South Pacific during World War II; Guadalcanal, Iowa Jima, Okinawa, etc. It was very exciting to see a military base up close and to hear a Marine talk about those famous battlegrounds.

We resumed our trip to New Jersey early the next morning. They lived at the time in Caldwell, New Jersey. Aunt Tish missed the exit off the Garden State Freeway we should have taken and found ourselves headed for Connecticut. She saw a police car on the shoulder of the highway and stopped to ask him if there was any way she could turn around before driving all the way to Connecticut. He waved her on without any offer of help.

To my surprise after pulling back onto the Freeway, I heard Aunt Tish say "I'll be d___ed if I'm going to drive all the way to Connecticut." She then proceeded to execute a U-turn across the median right there in front of the officer. To our relief, the officer didn't react in anyway. We finally made it safely to Caldwell.

I enjoyed my visit there very much. Among other trips, they took me to New York City one day. I had heard of New York City but had never dreamed I would be walking its streets one day. We went to Radio City Music Hall, saw a movie entitled "People Will Talk" starring Cary Grant and Jeanne Crain. We also saw a performance by the Rockettes. I had a lot to tell my friends back in Chinquapin and Wilmington when I returned.

My half-sister, Elna Maready Leonard, and her family were living in Pompton Lakes, a small town a few miles away. I stayed one night with her and her family. She had three children, Raymond, Pam, and Jeff. Her husband, Ray Leonard, had been an army pilot during World War II.

I was kind of sorry when the visit was over but I was looking forward to getting back to my family in Wilmington. It was only a few days before I would start my sophomore year at NHHS.

Aunt Tish had assured Mother the return trip on the Greyhound bus would be very easy. I didn't find it so. I was put on the bus in Caldwell, had to change in Newark,

Philadelphia, and in Richmond. Those bus stations were somewhat larger than the ones in Wallace and Wilmington. I stayed confused most of the time but with help from the friendly Greyhound staff, I finally arrived at the Wilmington bus terminal the next day, after having ridden all night.

With my suitcase in hand, I walked to Second and Princess Streets. There I caught the city bus that went to the Winter Park area. I got off the bus at the corner of Kerr and Wrightsville Avenues and walked up on the porch of our house. When I walked into the house, I was shocked to see the house was completely empty; no people and no furniture.

I went from room to room, upstairs and downstairs, calling out names but no one answered. There were no notes or notices anywhere. I went outside and sat down on the front steps and pondered my next move. Where could my family be? Had some gang of robbers and kidnappers come by and taken everybody and holding them for ransom?

After sitting there a few minutes, I decided I had to do something. It didn't look like my family would be coming back anytime soon. There was a small service station just across the road. I walked over there and spoke to the owner. I had been to his store a few times before I went to Chinquapin for the summer and he recognized me.

I nervously asked him "Do you know if anything happened to the family that lived across the street? There's not a single soul in the house and I looked everywhere."

"Well, sure," he answered. "There was a moving van there on Wednesday, Williams Moving Company, I think. I saw them load everything on the truck. I ain't seen no body back there since."

"Do you have any idea where they moved? I've been away for a few days and nobody told me they were moving while I was gone. I cain't believe they moved while I was away and nobody told me."

"Well, their littlest boy came over here to get a Pepsi that morning while they were loading and told me they were moving to a house somewhere on Fifth Avenue. He couldn't remember the number. I noticed his right arm was in a sling. What happened to him?"

"Nothing much," I answered. "Our cousin fell on him while we were playing football a few days ago. He's gonna be okay. He's pretty tough. Are you sure he said Fifth Avenue? That's a long street, ain't it?"

"Oh, yeah. It runs from Greenfield Park all the way to the northern edge of town. It's a pretty long street all right."

I thanked him and went back over to the house and sat down on the steps again and pondered some more. Finally, I decided I'd just have to get back on the city bus and ride to Fifth Avenue.

I got off the bus at the corner of Princess Streets and Fifth Avenue. I stood there for a few minutes trying to decide whether I should walk North or South, on the East side or the West side. I wasn't familiar with that area of Wilmington. I had lived in Riverside Apartments for five months and then in Winter Park for three months although I was in Chinquapin for most of that period.

I looked down the street and saw a great big church with a huge steeple. Out in the middle of the street, I could see a large water fountain. That direction seemed more interesting as opposed to walking north so I began walking that way. When I got to the water fountain, I could hardly believe the name on the historical marker, Kenan Memorial Fountain. I was surprised to see my name on such an impressive water foundation.

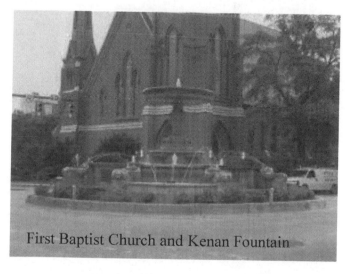

First Baptist Church and Kenan Fountain

With my suitcase in hand, I continued walking south on the east side of Fifth Avenue not really knowing what I was hoping to see. I crossed Market Street, then Dock Street, then Orange Street and was about to give up hope when I suddenly spied a familiar looking chair on the porch of a house near the corner of Fifth Avenue and Ann Streets. The address was 221 South Fifth Avenue. It was directly across the street from a really big church. I wasn't sure but the chair looked like one of our old chairs. I walked up on the porch and timidly knocked on the door.

To my surprise and relief, the lady who answered the knock was my Mother. I could hardly belief that just through pure luck, I had found my family. Miraculously, I had walked south rather than north and Mother had left an old chair on the porch. I was almost in tears I was so happy to be home. While I was trudging along Fifth Avenue, I had wondered if I would ever see my family again.

"What made y'all move without telling me?" I asked. "Why didn't you tell me before I left for New Jersey that you were planning to move? Were you trying to get rid of me?"

221 S. Fifth Avenue

Mother explained she realized living in Winter Park in such a nice house was more than she could afford even with Hoagy paying part of the rent. She had a first cousin, Alice Knowles, who told Mother about a very nice house just around the corner from her, on Fifth Avenue, that had just become available for rent and the rent was somewhat lower than the rent on the house at Winter Park.

Mother and Daddy went to look at the house and decided at once to take it. Gerald and Coleman would go to school at Tileston just across the street. Joan and I could walk to NHHS and save a little money on bus fare. So the decision to move and the move itself was done quickly. Mother persuaded our renters, Hoagy and Betty, to move with them.

She had written a letter to me, she said, while I was still in New Jersey about the move but it hadn't arrived when I started back home. Long-distance phone calls were completely out of the question in those days. I asked Aunt Tish and Aunt Adele sometime later if they remembered getting a letter from Mother about the move. They said no but they may have forgotten about it.

For many years afterwards, I felt that I needed closure with respect to the time my family ran away from home. I was left home alone.

Chapter 8
Sophomore Year at NHHS

I began my sophomore year in September, 1951. Babcock and Wilcox had just announced it was going to have a facility in Wilmington that would employ as many as 600 people. The Korean War, which began in June, 1950, was in its second year. The hit movie "Flying Leathernecks" starring John Wayne was showing at the Baily Theatre and according to the Personals Column in the Wilmington Star-News, "Mr. and Mrs. W. B. Creasy and son, Albert, have returned home after a week's visit in Washington, D. C., and New York City."

Joan and I were able to walk to NHHS, only eleven blocks away. My two friends, Vernon Meshaw and Leonard Williams, would often walk by my house and we would walk to school together. Vernon and his family lived at the corner of Second and Wright Streets and Leonard lived at Nesbitt Courts. They had a much longer walk than I did.

Gerald and Coleman went to Tileston, just across the street. Their first day was a little rough on them. Mother didn't know about the registration process. On opening day she told them to walk over to the school and somebody would tell them where to go. When they got there, they learned all the students were to sit in the auditorium and each teacher would call out the names of students that were assigned to that particular teacher. They sat next together for mutual support and continued to sit there until every student's name had been called except for them and another young boy, Bobby Hanchey.

They sat there, alone in the auditorium, for a few minutes, not knowing what to do. They conversed softly in frightened tones asking each other what should be their next step. Bobby Hanchey came over and sat with them, looking to them for leadership which they were not able to provide. Finally, the principal came into the auditorium, saw them sitting there, walked over, looked at them suspiciously, and asked them to identify themselves.

Being the oldest, Gerald spoke up. "Well, my name's Gerald Maready, this is my brother, Coleman, and I don't know what his name is," as he pointed to Bobby. "We just moved to 221 South Fifth Street and we thought we'd be going to school here but nobody's claimed us so far,"

The principal asked them to follow him to his office where he talked to his assistant for a few minutes as they looked over some enrollment sheets. At last, they found spots for Gerald, Coleman and Bobby and the assistant walked them to their respective rooms and introduced them to their teacher. As classes had already started, their entrance caused a disruption which caused their teacher to be ill-disposed to them. Or at least that was their opinion as they later recalled that day.

The walks in the morning to NHHS were enjoyable, especially if the weather was nice. If it was raining, or if it was cold, it was not so much fun. As we walked along, other NHHS students might join our group.

There were two or three students on the way who were in my home room. One of them, Sue Walton, lived about a block from me on 5th Avenue. She was a very pretty, friendly girl, but she must have had a ride as she never walked with us.

I desperately wanted to get a part-time job in the afternoons or evenings but just couldn't find one. I was still only 15 and couldn't get a work permit. Leonard, who was a year older, had an afternoon and weekend job at Mills Grocery at the corner of Third and Castle Streets.

Vernon earned some money by helping his Daddy and his older brother, Howard, in their scrap iron business. They drove around the country side in Mr. Meshaw's old truck, searching for old junked cars, trucks, appliances, etc. Their biggest customer was Queensboro Steel Co., located at Front and Wright Streets, very near Vernon's home.

Queensboro Steel was founded by the Alper brothers, Seymour and George, who moved to Wilmington in the early '50's from New York. Mr. Seymour Alper later chaired a committee that was responsible for the building of New Hanover Regional Medical Center.

Mother always wanted her children to attend Sunday School and church. As there was a large, beautiful church just across the street, she felt perhaps it would be good for her children to attend church there. She didn't know much about the Catholic religion as there were no Catholic churches in the Chinquapin area.

St. Mary's Catholic Church

It seemed to be a prosperous church with its size, its domed roof, and its turrets with what appeared to be embattlements. It also seemed to be a busy church, even on Saturday afternoons and evenings. Sunday was an especially busy day, with people coming and going all morning long.

One Easter Sunday morning, she insisted that I, Gerald and Coleman attend their morning service. Joan refused to go. Mother had observed the 11 AM service seemed to be the most popular so that's the service we were to first attend. We put on our best Sunday clothes, no brogans or overall pants, and walked across the street and through the huge, imposing doors. Right away, we noticed the interior of St. Mary's looked much different from the interiors of Chinquapin Presbyterian Church or Salem Baptist Church.

Gerald and Coleman kept bumping into the pews and tables as they couldn't seem to keep their eyes off the domed roof. It was magnificent and the stained glass windows in the alcoves were breath-taking. We weren't sure where to sit so we went down front as that is where Mother had always told us devout Christians should sit.

We were suddenly startled by a procession of people, elaborately costumed, walking slowly down the aisle towards the front. One man was carrying a cross as he walked behind the leader. When they finally reached the front, everyone sat down except for the preacher. He said something we didn't understand and everybody said "And also with you." He then said something else and everybody said "Amen."

At some point in the service, the preacher took a jar of water and walked up and down the aisle, throwing drops of water on everybody. Gerald and Coleman ducked when he tried to throw water on them. He went back to the front and said a few more things I couldn't understand. Each time he said something, everybody else would say "Lord have mercy," or "Amen," or "Thanks be to God."

Sometimes, after he said something, everybody would stand up and say something. I felt we should also stand up when everyone else did so I motioned for Gerald and Coleman to stand the next time. We never could get our timing right. By the time we stood, all the others sat down. When we sat down, everyone else stood up. Other worshipers began to look at us.

When we finally got out and went back across the street, we told Mother we didn't think we'd go back to the Catholic Church. The worship was too long and too complicated for us.

When Mother told her cousin, Alice Knowles, about our experience, Alice told us there was a small Baptist Church at the corner of Sixth and Ann, the Tabernacle Baptist Church. The name alone seemed right to us. "Tabernacle" and "Baptist" were comforting words to people from Chinquapin. I began to go there on a regular basis.

Tabernacle Baptist Church

It was a small white wood-framed building right across the street from Shepherd's Grocery at Sixth and Ann. Shepherd's Grocery, a small corner grocery store was where we bought most of our groceries while we lived at 221 South Fifth Street. The Shepherds had a son, B. J. Shepherd, who was a grade behind me. He was an outstanding athlete.[4]

---

[4] Shepard's Grocery was acquired by a classmate, Mike Poulos, much later. It burned down during the race riots of 1971. The Wilmington Ten were accused of setting the store on fire.

Chapter 9
Learning To Dance

The 1951 football season was an exciting one for NHHS students and fans. The opening game was an unexpected lopsided win over Greensboro, 40 – 0. Emo Boado, Burt Grant, Flo Worrell, Mack Overton, and Sonny Jurgensen starred in the one-sided contest.

During the regular season, the team won nine games and tied one. The Wildcats went on to win the 3-A state championship. At that time, the largest schools made up the 3-A classification. After winning the 3-A state championship, the Wildcats played a school from Concord, Massachusetts, in the Piedmont Bowl in Winston-Salem but lost 13-20. The team then played a team from Miami, Florida, in the Orange Bowl but lost 7-21.

High school football players were much smaller in the 1950's. Of the thirty-four players on the team, only three weighed more than 200 pounds. Emo Boado, the starting halfback, only weighed 143 pounds. The largest player was George Johnson who weighed 230 pounds.

I was able to save enough of my lunch money to go to some of the games at Legion Stadium. What fun that was! The games on Friday nights were followed by a dance at the Community Center at the corner of Second and Orange Streets. The only dancing I had ever done was a square dance at a barn raising or similar event in Chinquapin.

I was given an opportunity to learn to dance during some of my Physical Education classes at NHHS. We had to walk over to the girls' gym in the Isaac Bear Building occasionally for the purpose of learning to dance. Mrs. Jean Tillett, the girls' PE teacher, would pair off each boy with a girl, turn on the phonograph and away we would go. I was very short for my age and Mrs. Tillett had a knack for pairing me with girls who were several inches taller.

The songs were generally very slow and the boys had to hold their dancing partner around their waist as they glided across the floor. I was clumsy, awkward, and very nervous. My dancing partners seemed to have really long feet. Although I tried my best I couldn't help but step on them several times. We were also supposed to learn to make polite interesting conversation as we danced. Dancing and talking at the same time were beyond my capabilities.

Other boys were paired up with very pretty girls and they seemed to enjoy dancing: Ernest Anderson and Miriam Hickman, Pete Land and Karen Kurka, Tommy Millard and Gloria Smith, Harold Manning and Jackie Green, Jimmy Covil and Ann Croom and a bunch of others. They were better dancers than the teen-agers in Billy Brinkley's store in Chinquapin.

On my last trip to the girls' gym to learn to dance, I was assigned to a pretty girl who wasn't taller than me, Eula Craft. As I wasn't feeling uncomfortable about a size difference, I attempted some interesting conversation.

"You know, Eula, one thing I miss since moving to Wilmington from Chinquapin is nobody goes collard stealing down here. Have you ever been collard stealing?"

Eula looked at me with a questioning look and replied, "No, we just usually to the A & P to get our collards. Wasn't there an A & P in Chinquapin?"

"No, we just had Billy Brinkley's and Mr. Van Bradham's store and they didn't sell collards. Everybody grew their own."

"Well, if everybody grew their own, why did you go around stealing collards?"

I didn't have time to explain the intricacies about collard stealing on January 6th, the night of Old Christmas, so I decided to forget the interesting conversation and just concentrate on dancing. Luckily for her, Eula had small feet.

At the Community Center, the favorite dances seemed to be something called "The Bop," the "Hokey Pokey," or the "Bunny Hop." Some of the dancers liked the slow dances where their dancing partner was held close. Favorites were "Far Away Places," "Mona Lisa," "Too Young," and "Harbor Lights."

Chapter 10
Life on Fifth Avenue

Halloween was on Wednesday night in 1951, a school night. The kids in Wilmington did Halloween differently than we did in Chinquapin. In Chinquapin, we had never heard of "Trick or Treat." Our only goal on Halloween was to play tricks. No one invited me to go with them on Halloween night so I stayed home. Gerald and Coleman went out with a couple of their friends, Jerry Ellers and Tommy Powell.

Imagine my surprise and consternation when a group of young kids knocked on our door and yelled out "Trick or Treat" when I opened the door. I didn't know how to respond. I stared at them sternly until they slowly turned and ran away down the street. Gerald and his group came back shortly after and told me how much better Halloween was in Wilmington than in Chinquapin. He showed me a bag full of candy and small toys. "These people don't want tricks played on them so they give you a treat, usually candy," he said. "What a racket."

Even better than the candy was the treat a taxi driver gave to Gerald and his gang. He seemed to be asleep in his cab parked on Orange Street in front of Dr. George Koseruba's office. But as they walked by, he suddenly sat up and called them over. "Shay, kids, want a little treat?" He held up a half empty bottle of whiskey. They jumped back and were ready to run when he said, "Jush joking. I like your Halloween costumes, especially the one the little boy has on. I've alwaysh been a fan of Mickey Mouse. Here's a good treat for you,"

He reached down into a bag where he kept his fare money, pulled out a big handful of change and dropped it into Jerry's bag. "Now, mind you, split thish money up equ – equ – equ – fairly,"

Before he could change his mind, Gerald and his group ran off to Shepherd's Grocery. They went back into the rear of the store where they stooped down while Jerry divided the money. Their plan was to buy some candy after the money division.

"Here's one for you Tommy, here's one for you, Gerald, here's one for you, Coleman," he said as he dropped a coin into their bags. After a couple of rounds of dropping coins, Gerald noticed Jerry was dropping a dime or quarter into his own bag and that of Tommy while he dropped a penny or nickel into his and Coleman's bags.

"Here's a trick on you, Jerry," Gerald shouted. He grabbed the bag of coins from Jerry's hand and started to run out the store. Jerry caught him right in front of the cash register where Mr. Shepherd was standing. Jerry grabbed at the bag. It tore open and all the coins fell out onto the floor.

Mr. Shepherd exclaimed "What in the world? Where did you boys get all that money?" He asked as he looked down to make sure his money was still in the cash register drawer.

The tone of Mr. Shepherd's voice made Gerald and Jerry realize they should have settled their differences quietly. Gerald told him about the drunken taxi driver, parked in front of Dr. Koseruba's office, who had given them the bag of money as a Halloween treat.

"Why, that's old John Robinson. He shouldn't be giving away money. He owes me some right now for credit I've given him on his grocery bill. I believe y'all ort to give me the money and I'll get it back to him the next time he comes in. He was probably drunk and didn't really know what he was doing,"

They reluctantly gathered up all the coins, including the ones in their pockets, and handed them over to Mr. Shepherd. As they walked back home, Gerald and Jerry argued about whose fault it was that they had lost their money.

Later that evening, I began to understand what I was supposed to do when the kids came to the door. We didn't have any treats to give them. Joan and I had been eating some oranges and had a pile of orange peels. As the kids were asking for tricks or treats, we decided to give them tricks. We would put a handful of orange peels into the treat bags that were held up to us, being careful not to let them see what we were dropping into their bags. Some of them came back by later and threw their orange peels onto our front porch. Ingrates!

My oldest sister, Sudie, who was married in July, 1951, came to visit us for Thanksgiving. Our room renters, Hoagy, Betty, and Hoagy, Jr., were still with us. On Friday morning after Thanksgiving Day, Betty went outside to get in her car for a quick trip to the drug store. Imagine her surprise when her car wasn't where it was supposed to be, in front of the house. It was a 1944 Studebaker coupe with lots of rust and dents.

She came back in and consulted with us. It was obvious that someone had stolen her car. "Now, Betty," don't let yourself get upset," Sudie said to her. "We'll call the police and maybe they'll be able to recover your car."

"Hoagy's going to kill me when he gets back from Camp LeJeune this evening. He's told me lots of times I shouldn't leave the keys in the car. Who would steal an old car like that? They maybe want to use it as a getaway car when they rob a bank," Betty cried.

Sudie called the police for Betty and in a few minutes a police car pulled up in front of our house. When Sudie and Betty walked up to the police car, the driver rolled the left front window halfway down. A mean-looking German Police dog stuck his head out the window and snarled and barked fiercely at them. The closest police car to our home was a canine unit.

They walked around the car to the driver's side and gave him a description of Betty's car. Meanwhile, the dog continued his snarling and barking. The policeman decided they would ride around the area to look for the car. He told Sudie and Betty to get in the back seat. Sudie asked, "What about that dog? He wants to eat us up."

"Naah, don't worry about him. He's all bark and no bite." the policeman told them. "I've got him under control. But be sure you don't make any sudden moves back there. He don't like sudden moves."

They got in but sat as close to the left rear door as they could, almost on top of each other. Once they were in the dog stopped snarling and barking but kept his eye on them in case they made any sudden moves.

They had only ridden four or five car lengths when the police car stopped and the driver asked, "Don't that look like your car right there," as he pointed to a car parked along the curb.

"Well, I'll be," Betty exclaimed. "That is my car"! She was embarrassed to reveal the truth. When she parked her car the previous night there wasn't room in front of our house so she had driven a few car lengths up Fifth Street and parked there. She had forgotten where she parked and assumed she left the car directly in front of our house as she always did.

Ain't that funny?" Betty asked. The policeman was not amused. He asked Betty and Sudie to get out of the car and in a loud, rude voice told Betty to keep up with her car in the future and not waste his time.

"Well, I declare," Sudie said. "You could be a little more polite. We ort to report you to your sergeant."

Upon hearing her angry tone of voice, the dog began snarling and barking louder than before and tried to climb out the half-open window. They ran back into the house and the canine unit police car drove off.

Chapter 11
The All American Redheads

Basketball was always my favorite sport. Back in Chinquapin, I had listened to every game North Carolina State played. It had so many great players: Dick Dickey, Sammy Ranzino, Bob Speight, Lee Terrill, and Vic Bubas. Their coach, Everett Case, was a basketball legend in North Carolina in the late '40's and early '50's.

I had thoughts of trying out for the junior varsity team but everyone told me I was too short. Instead, I formed a team with some of my school friends and we played in the City League at the Community Center at Second and Orange Streets. I named our team the Wolverines. I had read wolverines were extremely ferocious and would attack even larger animals. The Wolverine team stayed together for three years until we graduated.

As each of us wanted to play the entire game, we usually only had six team members. Mainstay team members were me, Vernon Meshaw, Leonard Williams, Marvin Watson, Jimmy Pappas, Joe Tardugno, and George Johnson, Jr., a small boy for his age, who had moved to Wilmington from Kentucky. He lived with his mother in an upstairs apartment on Orange Street between Second and Third. He was a little strange but had a great left-handed hook shot

The Community Center, on the corner of Second and Orange Streets, was only four blocks away from our home on Fifth Avenue. Located immediately behind the Community Center at Front and Orange Streets was the Merita Bakery. Sometimes I would walk past the Community Center and stand outside the Bakery just to smell the delicious aroma emanating from it.

I spent every available moment there after school playing basketball or ping-pong. It was a great place to hang out. There were some outstanding ping-pong players there; some of them state champions or runners up: Gary Preston, Paul Pappas, Bonnie Shain, Shuney Potter, and Zalma Brower to mention a few.

Zalma had won both the singles and doubles events in the intermediate division in a tournament in High Point earlier in 1951.

Everyone was looking forward to the beginning of the basketball season at NHHS. The opening game was played on December 6, 1951, against a touring group of lady professional players, known as the "All American Redheads." They were not your normal size girls, many of them were over six feet tall. One of them, Ruth Harms, owned a single game scoring record of 102 points.

The Redheads were favored to win not only because of their skill but because several boys who would normally be starters were in Winston-Salem where NHHS was playing Concord High School in the annual Piedmont Bowl Game.

To everyone's surprise, the Wildcats trounced the Redheads, 52 – 32. Starters for NHHS were George Gaddy, John Gerdes, Pete Peterson, Russell Clark and Harry Hayes. George was the leading scorer with twenty points.

Vernon and I had walked to see the game. We were surprised but happy our Wildcats had beaten a bunch of red-headed girls. "You know, them redheads weren't as good as they're cracked up to be," I told Vernon on our way home. "If our second string players can beat them, maybe the

Wolverines could have. With your jump shot and George's left handed hook, I believe we would have won,"

Vernon ran up the sidewalk a few steps, took an imaginary jump shot at an imaginary goal and said "Swish. Two more points for Meshaw. That makes 21 for tonight. Take that, you redheads," By that time, we had reached my home at on Fifth Street. I went inside while Vernon walked on. He still had nine more blocks to go in the cold.

The NHHS Wildcats didn't have as good a season as they usually did. Their regular season record was nine wins and three losses. Our only consolation was they had beaten the All-American Redheads.

The team was in Winston-Salem on December 22nd and 23rd playing in a tournament. On the way home through High Point, Coach Leon Brogden was cited for running a traffic light. He had to pay a ten dollar fine and court costs. I expect that was the only time in his life Coach Brogden ever violated any law.

In the state tournament, the Wildcats won their first game but lost in overtime in their second game to the eventual winner of the tournament, Hugh Morson High School in Raleigh. Flo Worrell was named to the All-State First Team.

Many of the starters on the school sports teams played all three major sports: football, basketball, and baseball: Julian Rogers, Burt Grant, Sonny Jurgensen, Emo Boado, Rex Hardy, Mack Overton, Flo Worrell, and George Gaddy.

They seemed so competent in all sports I could only watch and envy them; they were my heroes. Not only did I greatly admire these sports heroes, but I had great admiration for some other senior boys who were Big Men On Campus: Billy West, Jimmy Ingram, Richard Rogers, Paul Burton, and David Padrick. They seemed so sophisticated. I wanted to be like them when I grew up, or got to be a Senior, whichever came first.

Chapter 12
Shopping in Downtown Wilmington

In early December, 1951, Mother applied for a job at the Belk-Beery store. To her surprise, she was hired. Mother had never worked outside the house before other than at the tobacco barn in the summer and at hog-killings.

She was assigned to the gift-wrapping section. With Christmas fast approaching, the management at Belk's was anticipating a huge demand for wrapping Christmas gifts. Mother seemed to enjoy her work. It was an entirely different experience for her. She had to help the customers select the size box they needed, the kind of wrapping paper they wanted, and the type bow they desired.

She was really happy to have that extra income. It allowed her to buy a few little things for the house and for herself. She hoped she would be able to get a part-time job for me and Joan at Belk's, but that didn't work out.

Belk-Beery's Department Store was a fabulous place. The store had moved a year or two earlier from its location at 232 North Front Street. There were three floors with escalators and elevators going to each floor. There wasn't anything like that in Chinquapin.

At Christmas, people would flock from everywhere to look into the huge display window at the main entrance. The Christmas scenes were incredible; automated characters, Santa, Rudolph, elves, reindeer, with snow softly falling. It was a magical place.

Mother usually got off work at 6 PM and had to walk to our house on Fifth Street, a walk of eight blocks. Often times I walked to Belk's, waited for her to get off work and then walked back to our house with her. Sometimes Gerald and Coleman would go with me.

While we waited, they liked to play hide 'n seek in the store, running from floor to floor, or riding the elevator or escalator up and down. Some of their friends may walk with us to the store and would join in the game. The result was a herd of little boys running wild in the store. Mr. Bill Beery caught them on two or three occasions and asked them to go outside and play. He seemed to understand boys liked to have fun but he would rather they have fun outside his store.

Before Mother got the job at Belk's, we had mostly shopped at Efird's Department Store, corner of Front and Grace Streets. It was a huge department store with three floors. The most interesting thing about Efirds's was the system used to take the customer's money and return any change. The clerk would place the sales ticket and the customer's money into a cannister which would be placed into a tube and, "whisk," the cannister was sucked off into some far-off office where a cashier would look at the sales ticket and then count out the proper amount of change. She would then put the sales ticket and the change back into the cannister and put it back into the tube and, "whisk," the cannister was returned to the sales clerk.

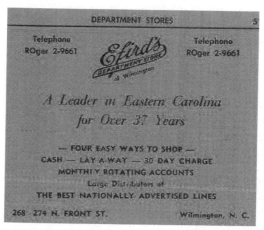

I was fascinated by this system. Billy Brinkley's store in Chinquapin could have used it on Saturday nights. There were tubes all over the store with cannisters whizzing back and forth all day. There was also an elevator in Efird's that was operated for the convenience of customers by an elevator operator. You would step into the elevator; the operator would ask "What floor, please?" And up or down you would go.

Downtown Wilmington was where you had to go back in the early '50's if you wanted to shop. All of the chain stores were downtown as well as most large local businesses.

Rhodes Furniture	18 S. Front St.
MacMillan & Cameron Co.	3rd & Chestnut
J. C. Penney	243 N. Front St.
Sutton Council Furniture	313 N. Front St.
Sears, Roebuck	307 N. Front St.
Crystal Restaurant	26 N. Front St.
H & W Cafeteria	118 Princess St.
Friendly Cafeteria	111 Chestnut St.
Dixie Restaurant	115 Princess St.
Cape Fear Ford Motor Sales	215 Market St.
Nonesuch Restaurant	123 Market St.
Puritan Restaurant	133 Market St.
Jiffy Grill	306 N Front St.
The Groceteria Grocery Store	127 Market St.
Walgreen's Drug Store	226 N Front St.

Chapter 13
NHHS Extra Curricular Activities

Student Government was an important aspect of the culture of NHHS. Elections were held early in the fall and electioneering was very spirited.

Other NHHS students were very active even if they weren't involved in Student Government, football or basketball. In early December, 1951, the annual Declamation Contest was underway. The students who participated in this contest had to recite some piece of oratory or poem while acting out the sense of the piece. The eventual winners were Nathan Skipper, Helen Williams and Jerry Tureen

It was wondrous to me students my own age could get up in front of the entire student body and give a performance that was worthy of an Oscar.

Another very popular event in early December was the performance of what was called the "Womanless Fashion Show," Barbara Hatcher was the leader of the group who put this remarkable performance together.

The boys who embarrassed themselves greatly by pretending to be female fashion models were: Ashton Godley,

Bobby Tate, Al Gumb, Joe Hood, W. T. Bradshaw, Wiley Brown, and Billy Costas.

The swimming team practiced and had its home meets at the YMCA swimming pool. The YMCA was located on the North East corner of Third and Market Streets.

Coach Smith represented the United States at the 1924 Summer Olympics in Paris. He competed in the men's 1,500 meter freestyle, advanced to the semifinals, and posted a time of 22 minutes and 39 seconds. Johnny Weissmuller was also on the American team in that Olympics. He won three gold medals in swimming and one in bronze in water polo. Mr. Weissmuller later became famous for his role as Tarzan in twelve motion pictures.

1951 Top Songs, Movies and Books
Top Ten Songs
 Too Young by Nat King Cole
 Because of You by Tony Bennett
 How High The Moon by Les Paul and Mary Ford
 Come On-a My House by Rosemary Clooney
 Be My Love by Mario Lanza
 On Top of Old Smoky by The Weavers
 Cold, Cold Heart by Tony Bennett
 If by Perry Como
 Loveliest Night of the Year by Mario Lanza
 Tennessee Waltz by Patti Page

Top Five Movies
 Quo Vadis with Robert Taylor & Deborah Kerr
 Alice in Wonderland with Kathryn Beaumont
 Show Boat with Kathryn Grayson & Howard Keel
 Streetcar Named Desire with Marlon Brando & Vivien Leigh
 David and Bathsheba with Gregory Peck & Susan Hayward

Top Five Best Selling Books
 From Here to Eternity by James Jones
 The Caine Mutiny by Herman Wouk
 Moses by Sholem Asch
 The Cardinal by Henry Morton Robinson
 A Woman Called Fancy by Frank Yerby

Chapter 14
Life in Dry Pond

After living at 221 South Fifth St. for a few months, Mother decided it was time for us to move again. The family that rented a room from us had moved away and we could no longer afford such a nice house.

I never was sure how Mother selected some of the houses we moved into. I did know which moving company she would select to move us. Gerald had a friend, Eddie Williams, whose father owned a small moving company, Williams Moving Company. We must have been his best customer as we moved six times in four years.

This move, in early 1952, was to 408 Church Street, the downstairs apartment. The house, built in 1861, was owned by an elderly lady, Miss Cornelia Brady. Miss Brady lived in the upstairs apartment.

408 Church St.

Miss Brady was a gentle Southern lady. She was quiet, courteous, and helpful. She never bothered anyone. My family, with four children and visiting friends, may have put a strain on her tranquility. She was a devout member of the First Baptist Church.

Miss Brady had some beautiful azaleas around her house at 408 Church St. The flowers began blooming in full just after we moved in. This yard looked much better than the yard at our house in Chinquapin. It even looked better than the yard at 4409 Wrightsville Avenue.

That area of Wilmington was known as Dry Pond. A lot of my friends and classmates, as well as friends and classmates of my sister, Joan, and my brothers, Gerald and Coleman, lived in the area. South Fourth Street seemed to have an inordinate number of teen-age children in the early '50's. It was a great community in which to live.

Hall's Drug Store was considered to be the capital of Dry Pond. Other well-known businesses were Drake's Bakery at Fourth and Castle, Joe's Market at Fourth and Nun, Southside Drug Store at Front and Castle, and Sneeden's Food Store at 407 South Fourth St.

Having lived in two areas with colorful names, Mill Swamp near Chinquapin, and Dry Pond, I believe Dry Pond offered the most educational and recreational opportunities. If you have to live in a swamp or a pond, it's better to be able to keep your feet dry.

Chapter 15
My First Azalea Festival - 1952

This was the first year in Wilmington that I gave much thought to the Annual Azalea Festival. In 1951, we lived in Riverside Apartments and didn't really know anything about it. The first year of the Festival was 1948 so 1952 was only its fifth year. The Wilmington Star-News was full of upcoming festival events.

Cathy Downs, movie actress, was the Azalea Queen. She was a last-minute replacement for Gloria De Haven. For some reason, never put into the paper, Miss De Haven, cancelled out.

The Parade Marshall was William Rehder. Several football stars would ride in the parade including Charlie Justice, Eddie

LeBaron and Otto Graham. The parade would have forty-four floats and twenty-three bands.

Leonard and I planned to walk down to the parade site early in order to get a good viewing site. He came by my house and as we were leaving, Mother told me I would have to let Gerald and Coleman go with us. They wanted to see the parade and she couldn't go with them. I grudgingly assented.

I was eager to see a really big parade. I loved to see the bands as they marched along, playing some patriotic song, with the drum major and the majorettes strutting in front of the band. I had been to see the Strawberry Festival Parade in Wallace once or twice but I anticipated the Azalea Festival Parade might be even better than the Wallace parade.

As we got close to the reviewing stand in front of City Hall, we could hear some country music. There was a band at the top of the stand playing the "Guitar Boogie," a song made famous by Arthur Smith and the Crackerjacks. I couldn't believe I would be that close to the Crackerjacks so I approached some man standing at the bottom of the stand.

"Excuse me, sir," I said. "Who's that up yonder playing?"

"Why, that's Arthur Smith and the Crackerjacks. They're going to be playing here for 'bout half an hour, until the Parade starts," he answered.

"C'mon boys, let's get up close to the band. This is the chance of a lifetime," I said and started to walk up the steps of the stand. We hadn't got far when some big man wearing a nice green sports coat jumped in our way and said "Let's see your tickets."

"Tickets, what tickets," I asked. "I thought this was free."

"You can hear the music free from down on the street but this stand is only for festival celebrities and you boys don't look like celebrities," the man said. "Get on back down from here before you bump into one of our celebrities."

As the man was pushing us back down the steps, Leonard yelled up to the Crackerjacks. "Hey, Mr. Arthur, can you tell this man to let us get up there with you?"

Mr. Smith pretended he couldn't hear. He cupped his left ear with his hand and shook his head, never missing a note in the "Guitar Boogie". By this time, we were back down on the street. Leonard decided to give up. He was upset with Arthur Smith and walked off but Gerald, Coleman and I stood there and listened to the Crackerjacks for almost thirty minutes. I enjoyed his music even more than Home Briarhopper and the Dixie Dudes.

The parade was much more than I expected. Forty-four floats and twenty-three bands can put on quite a performance. My favorite was the NHHS band with Ronald Hailey as the drum major and Thelma Barclift, Jean Wagamon, Linda Pridgen, Ellen Whitley, Carolyn Cole and Judy Malpass.as majorettes.

Leonard and I got as far out in the street as we could get when the convertible with Eddie LeBaron, Otto Graham, and Charlie Justice rode by. "Hey, Choo Choo, catch this pass," Leonard yelled and pretended to throw a football to Mr. Justice. He pretended to throw the ball back and I jumped in front of Leonard and pretended to catch it. It was the only pretended pass I ever pretended to catch thrown by a professional football player.

The last float was the one with the Azalea Queen, Cathy Downs, and the Teen-Age Princess, Mary Catherine White, and her court. He yelled out to her, "Hey, Mary Catherine, throw me a kiss." Leonard wasn't hesitant about yelling out at people to get their attention.

Mary Catherine held up her gloved right hand and waved in our general direction. Leonard was overjoyed. He took it as a direct response to his request.

In connection with the Azalea Festival, the city also had a golf tournament each year, the Azalea Open. In 1952, the winner of the tournament was Jimmy Clark who won the top prize of $2,000.00.[5]

On the evening before the day of the parade, an informal street dance was held in the shopping area of Sixteenth and Market Streets, beginning at 9 PM. Two bands provided the music: Bobby Haas and his thirteen piece orchestra followed by Jack Pate's Rhythmairs, a seven piece band. Market Street was closed to traffic during the hours of the street dance.

Chapter 16

I Join First Baptist Church

One of the most important events in my life happened that spring. Miss Brady was a devout Christian who attended First Baptist Church regularly. She had told Mother many times she wished her children would attend Sunday School at her church. I was going to Sunday School sporadically at Tabernacle Baptist church but not enough to serve as a Christian role model for anyone.

One evening two men rang our door bell and identified themselves as deacons at First Baptist Church. When Gerald and Coleman heard them mention they were from a church, they ran back to the kitchen at the very back of the house. They were afraid the visitors were from the Catholic Church.

Mother wasn't at home at the time so I had to face the music alone. The men were friendly but very serious about their purpose in visiting us. They talked to me at length about

---

[5] Arnold Palmer won the Azalea Open in 1957. First prize was $1,700.00.

my salvation and the urgent need for me to join a church, more specifically, their church. After about a half-hour, I acceded to their suggestion and agreed to meet them at the worship service at First Baptist the next Sunday.

I told Mother what had happened when she returned and she seemed happy I had made that kind of decision.

When the next Sunday came, I thought I had a headache and shouldn't get out of the house but Mother held me to my promise to the two deacons. So I walked the five blocks to the church and was standing outside at Fifth and Market Streets, admiring the sign that identified the fountain as Kenan Memorial Fountain, when the two deacons found me.[6]

They guided me into the sanctuary and we sat down in the second pew from the front, right in front of the pulpit. I had never been into such a magnificent church before with the possible exception of St. Mary's Catholic Church. The carpet, the stained glass windows, the woodwork, and the huge chandeliers were beautiful. The Sharon Baptist Church in Chinquapin paled in comparison.

The Reverend Randolph Gregory, dressed in a black robe, delivered the sermon in a sonorous voice. At the conclusion of the sermon, he came down from his pulpit and said: "During our final hymn, if there is anyone here today that has never accepted Christ as their savior or if there is anyone here who feels led to join our church, please come forward as the hymn is sung,"

The choir, which was seated way up over the pulpit in a balcony kind of structure, began to sing the hymn of invitation "*Just As I Am.*" When they began the second verse, one of my deacons took my arm and whispered "It's time to go." I shrank back but he was determined I shouldn't back out. He finally sort of pulled me to my feet and gave me a push towards Reverend Gregory, who didn't seem that happy to see me come forward. When people joined the church in Chinquapin, the pastor always seemed overjoyed his sermon had won another convert.

---

[6] The fountain was given by William R. Kenan, Jr. in 1921 in honor of his parents, Captain William R. Kenan, a Civil War veteran, and his wife, Mary Hargrave Kenan.

I was hoping the church congregation wouldn't vote me in but surprisingly there wasn't a single "Nay" vote when Reverend Gregory asked for a vote. After the service, he asked me to come over to the church on Tuesday evening at six P.M. at which time he would baptize me.

I showed up at the appointed time. The Reverend Gregory and my two deacons were waiting for me inside the church. I was put into the proper baptismal attire and in a few minutes, on May 25, 1952, I was a baptized member of the First Baptist Church.

Although I attended Sunday School sporadically, I wasn't a faithful member until I moved back to Wilmington after serving in the US Air Force and graduating from Wake Forest University in 1964. Over those many years, I often wondered why my baptism was done in the presence of only two witnesses. To my knowledge, all baptisms at First Baptist Church were always done during a Sunday morning or Sunday evening worship service. For many years, I felt I needed an explanation from the church staff as to why my baptism was different. For a long time, I felt that I needed closure on this meaningful event in my life.

New members of First Baptist Church were urged to attend some classes to learn the history of the church. I learned that the church was first organized in 1808. In 1833, the church building was located at Front and Ann Streets. The sanctuary at Fifth Avenue and Market Streets was constructed during the Civil War and completed in May, 1870.

It was a difficult time to raise money to build such a magnificent church during the Civil War. However, church members were determined to not let such a little thing as a war stop construction. During the war when the Union and the Confederacy were doing their best to annihilate each other, the pastor of the church solicited contributions from Northern churches and they responded generously.

During its long history, the church began several mission churches in the Wilmington area; one of them being Temple Baptist Church at 17th and Market Streets. About the same time I joined the First Baptist Church, Temple Baptist Church suffered a horrendous loss when a fire destroyed the building. Several NHHS students attended church there.

Fire Chief Ludie Croom reported the fire apparently started from an overheated furnace in the basement. The janitor of the church started a fire in the furnace and went about his duties. A Marine happened to pass by about 7:23 AM, noticed the smoke and called the fire department. But it was too late to save the church.

The church members rolled up their sleeves and on October 9, 1953, moved into their new sanctuary at the corner of 18th and Market Streets.

Chapter 17
NHHS Social Life

NHHS was recognized as one of the top high schools in North Carolina. Mr. Dale K. Spencer, principal, Mr. Fred Capps, Dean of Boys, and all the teachers expected students to always do their best, academically and morally. They insisted students always adhere to a high level of integrity.

However, some students found time to have a rather extended social life. The Wilmington Morning Star and the Wilmington News published a column every day written by students at NHHS about activities by students. Those NHHS reporters included Irene Emory, Sherry Rich, Edith Darden, Patsy Barrett, and Nancy and Ann Bruce.

Most of the daily reports contained news about dances, birthday parties, sleep-overs, travel, attendance at sports events, downtown shopping, going to movies, etc.

The Community Center building at Second and Orange Streets was used quite often by students; both for meetings to plan events and for events. The Center was managed by Mr. Fred Singleton who was very receptive to students using his facility.[7] One of the more important events at the Community Center was the dance after every home football game on Friday nights.

On the Center's bulletin board, Miss Gretchen Thomas, director, posted each Friday night several photos of couples dancing. If you could identify yourself in one of the photos,

---

[7] Mr. Singleton's daughter, Betty, was a student at NHHS.

Community Center

Another facility that was used very often by NHHS students was a place named White's Lodge. It was located near the North East Cape Fear River in Castle Hayne. It was built originally by Mr. E. L. White, owner of White's Ice Cream and Milk Company. Over the years, Mr. White allowed NHHS students to use his facility for whatever need they had; mostly birthday parties and dances.

Even the Wilmington papers would, on occasion, have a news article about a birthday party for one of the students. Here's an example of the newspaper articles that reported on birthday parties:

16ʰ Birthday Celebration Given to Fete Sue Walton

"Mr. and Mrs. A. B. Walton were hosts at White's Lodge on Saturday evening in compliment to their daughter, Miss Sue W. Walton on her sixteenth birthday, March 8, 1952.

Miss Walton, who received guests with her parents, wore a lovely gown of green taffeta and a pink carnation corsage tied with silver ribbon.

The ballroom was decorated with Southern smilax and ivy. A cover of white lace was used on the refreshment table which was centered with a crystal punch bowl encircled with ivy. Lighted green tapers were used in crystal holders, flanking the birthday cake and dishes were filled with nuts, mints and small decorated cakes.

Each guest received a small St. Patrick's Day corsage containing shamrocks, hats and pipes.

Dancing was enjoyed during the evening by approximately 200 friends of Miss Walton. Chaperones were Mr. and Mrs. Walton, Mrs. J. Reid Crawford, Anne Crawford, Mrs. A. C. Devine and Jeanne Walton."

In the Wilmington News on March 11, 1952, Sherry Rich reported on Sue Walton's birthday in Teen Times:

"Sharing in birthday honors this past weekend was Sue Walton, who staged a huge party on Saturday night at White's Lodge. Looking very sweet sixteen in a pretty blue dress and a fragrant corsage, she was seen greeting such guests as: Bunky Green, Joe Norwood, Patti Moore, Roxana Mebane, Jimmy Council, Adele Mann, William Furchess, Shirley Council, John Brindell, Margaret Thompson, Tommy Capps, Beth White, Kenneth Murphy, Miriam Hickman, Henry Gore, Irene Emory, and Richard Rogers.

Quite outstanding for the occasion was the St. Patrick's corsage consisting of shamrocks, green hats, and pipes: these were presented to each guest as they arrived.

Claude Efird, Graham Farmer, Liz Ann Ellis, Glen Avery, Edna Lee Lennon, Bobby Johnston, Anne Lassiter, Emerson Head, Ray Asbury, Louise Saunders, Jim Rivenbark, Bradford Murray, and Leo Thompson were particularly pleased with this original idea and were heard urging their friends to hurry and get one.

Refreshments were naturally delicious and consisted of punch, cake, mints, and peanuts. Some of the first ones seen in line included: Jim Loughlin, Jim Spivey, Bob Coleman, Albert Creasy, Bob Godley, Lennox Cooper, Alex Efird, Larry Bullard, George Lewis, Douglas Upchurch, Butch Craft, and Jerry Partrick.

Local talent, namely David Block, Van King and John Martin entertained with piano selections which everyone enjoyed. Time finally came to call it a night but what a grand night it was,"

On my 16th birthday in 1952, I had two invited guests, Vernon and Leonard. We went over to Drake's Bakery at the corner of Fourth and Castle Streets and ate a doughnut, while the jukebox played *"Tell Me Why"* by the Four Aces. My celebration wasn't written up in the Wilmington Star News, the Wilmington News, Teen Scene or Teen-Age Tattler.

Chapter 18
Back to Chinquapin

When school was over in May, 1952, I hadn't been able to find a job anywhere. I really needed to do something to earn some money to help Mother as she struggled to meet our living expenses. My only working experience was working in tobacco. She agreed with me I should go to Chinquapin to see if I could find a family that needed someone to crop tobacco that summer.

One day in late June, Harrell James and I hitchhiked to Chinquapin. It took us about three hours to reach Wallace. All our rides were very short, five or ten miles at the most. We walked several miles in between the rides.

Hitchhiking from Wallace to Chinquapin turned out to be easy. We had barely taken our hitchhiking position on Highway 41 out of Wallace when someone pulled up in a 1948 Fraser Manhattan. It was an old friend of mine, Jeff Futreal. Jeff was the son of Jim Futreal, the Duplin County deputy sheriff who served the Chinquapin area. We were glad to see him.

Jeff said as we roared off towards Chinquapin, "I ain't seen you in quite a while, Kenan. I think it was last summer the last time. Didn't you stay with Riley Dail and his family and help him put in his tobacco crop?"

"Yeah, I did and to tell the truth that's why I'm heading for Chinquapin today," I said. "Do you know anybody that might be looking for somebody to help in cropping tobacco this season?"

We were about to cross the bridge at the old water mill just before reaching Tin City. "Hey, Jeff, don't you think you should slow down a little for the bridge?" I yelled at him.

The bridge had been designed so it was elevated two or three feet above the level of the highway. The incline on both sides of the bridge was pretty steep. Unless you wanted to be thrown up against the roof of your car, you needed to slow down to about twenty miles an hour.

Jeff answered "Naah, I like to see how fast I can cross this bridge. This old car takes the bump better than any I've ever been in."

As we came off the bridge, both Harrell and I bounced off our seats with our heads striking the roof of the car. Jeff, who was holding onto the steering wheel with both hands didn't fly as high as we did. To my surprise and relief, the Manhattan survived the bump without any noticeable damage.

"Well, I'll be John Brown," Jeff said. "Daddy was talking yesterday about how hard it's been to line up some good croppers to help us this summer. Seem like everybody we used last year cain't help us this year. If you ain't in a hurry, when we get home, I believe Daddy would want to talk to you."

This was good news to me. I knew the family well, especially Jeff's younger brother, Clyde, whose nickname was "Toogie." Toogie was one year younger than me. Things worked out great. Mr. Futreal was happy to have me stay with them during the entire tobacco season. Downtown Chinquapin was in easy walking distance from their house. Toogie and Jeff were good friends of mine.

An extra benefit to the arrangement was that Toogie, only 15 years old, was the projectionist at the Hula Drive-in Theatre. Every day after finishing our farm work and eating supper, Toogie and I would walk over to the theatre. I had something interesting to do every night. It wasn't like staying at Riley Dail's house where there was nothing to do. The last movie usually ended about 10 o'clock so we weren't up real late. That was good because we had to get up around 5:30 every morning to take care of that tobacco waiting in the field for us.

I really enjoyed that summer even if cropping tobacco five or six days a week was extremely hard work. At night, I could get in the Hula free of charge because of my relationship with Toogie. There were always friends of mine at the theatre, either in their cars or in the Chicken House. Normally, there would be some girls in the Chicken House with whom I could have interesting conversations on the back row.

However, if Mr. Delmas Cottle, school janitor, and part-time Chicken House monitor, caught couples having interesting conversations, he would shine his huge flashlight on them. "Cut that out right now or I'm gonna tell your parents." That usually put a halt to the conversations.

Hula Drive-In

The summer of 1952 was the first time I ever went on a real date. Jeff could use his father's car for his dates. One Saturday morning I was told by Jeff if I could get a date we could go with him and his date, Dorothy Halso, that night to the movie in Wallace. I never had a date before and was a little apprehensive.

In the afternoon while enjoying the juke box music at Billy Brinkley's, Yvonne Sandlin happened to come in. I had flirted with her on past occasions in the Chicken House. I was very nervous but finally summoned up my courage and asked if she would go with Jeff and me and Dorothy to the movie in Wallace that night. To my great surprise, she said she would. I hardly knew what to say next.

Nonetheless, we worked out the details and on Saturday night, August 9, 1952, I went on my first date. I was almost sixteen years old and thought I was growing up at last.. The movie was "*The Road to Bali*," starring Bob Hope and Bing Crosby. Those two could really act.

For some reason, I became addicted to Dr. Pepper that summer. I would drink them out in the tobacco fields rather than Pepsi-Cola, my lifetime favorite. I would drink one or two during the movie at the Hula. I lived by their slogan *""Drink a bite to eat at 10, 2, and 4. Dr. Pepper's the friendly Pepper-Upper."* After getting back to Wilmington in August, I never wanted to taste Dr. Pepper again.

In addition to drinking a lot of Dr. Peppers that summer, I also ate a lot of cucumbers. Mr. and Mrs. Futreal seemed to have an inordinate need to go out of town on weekends. That left Jeff, Toogie, and me to fend for ourselves with respect to preparing meals. Neither of us was adept at that culinary art so we usually did the easiest thing to find off hunger. Cucumbers were plentiful, easy to peel, and tasted pretty good when sprinkled with salt and soaked in vinegar. They were our primary source of nourishment on most weekends.

Chapter 19
Head Usher at the Baily Theatre

I came back from Chinquapin in late August, 1952. I was now 16 years of age and about to enter the eleventh grade at NHHS. I really needed a job to help our home financial situation.

I had a good friend, Jimmy Pappas, whose father was the Pastor at the Greek Orthodox Church, corner of Second and Orange Streets, across from the Community Center. Jimmy and I were team members on the Wolverines, a basketball team that played in the city Youth League. Jimmy's brother, Paul, was an outstanding ping-pong player and had won several championships. Both Jimmy and Paul spent a lot of time at the Community Center as they lived just across the street.

Jimmy was working as an usher at the Bailey Theatre and wanted to help me get an usher's job. I went with him one day to the Bailey where he introduced me to Mr. Gus Grist, the manager. After a grueling interview, Mr. Grist approved my application. I was to be paid thirty-five cents an hour.

I started to work the following Wednesday. There were five walk-in theatres then: the Baily, the Bijou, the Manor, the Carolina, and the Ritz, a theatre on North Fourth Street that served the black community. The Bailey was a top of the line theatre.

The ushers wore dark blue pants and a short light gray jacket that ended at the waist. The uniform was topped off with a white cardboard dickey and a black bow tie.

There were at least two ushers on duty at all times. One usher collected tickets from patrons that had been purchased at the outside ticket booth. Some ushers didn't tear the tickets in half but would save one or two for friends to use later on. One or two ushers stood at the head of the two aisles and with the aid of a flashlight help the patrons find an empty seat.

Bailey Theatre

In addition to the main floor, the Bailey also had a very nice balcony where young couples liked to sit, especially on the back row where they thought wouldn't be seen. There was also a second balcony where black patrons sat. They had a separate entrance, a separate ticket booth, and a separate snack counter. Segregation was still strictly observed in those days.

The Bailey Theatre and the Bijou Theatre were owned by the Autry family. While the Bailey was renowned for its class, the Bijou was renowned for its character. It featured mostly Grade B movies with occasional serials and cartoons thrown in. On Saturday afternoons, the Bijou would be filled with yelling, scrambling, and tussling younger kids. Empty flattened popcorn boxes were often seen sailing through the air. The movie screen had several tears in it as a result of the flying popcorn boxes.

If during the showing of a movie at any of the other theatres, something happened to disrupt the showing, you would hear cries of "Bijou," "Bijou," coming from the audience. The Bijou had a reputation, richly deserved, of having several breakdowns during the showing of their movies.

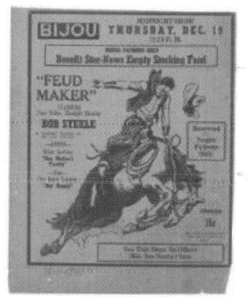

Other teen-age boys who worked as an usher at the Baily during my time there were: Jimmy Pappas, Jimmy Covil, Floyd Gore, Eddie Kraus, Bobby Britt and Winston Thompson.

Generally, I worked five evenings and nights at the Baily. I also worked on most Saturday and Sunday afternoons.

Movies typically began a run on Sunday and ran through Tuesday. Another movie would begin on Wednesday and run through Saturday night.

After working there for a few months, Mr. Grist called me into his office one evening and asked if I would like to be the head usher. Jimmy Covil, who had been the head usher, decided to retire from the usher life and seek greener pastures elsewhere. I had never aspired to such a high office. In the back of my mind, I had a goal of finding a job sometime that would provide me with a skill that would enable me to earn a decent living. I wasn't sure the skills I learned as an usher in a movie theatre would meet my requirements.

Mr. Grist explained to me at length the responsibilities of the head usher. After describing them to me, he concluded his interview by saying "And your rate of pay will be increased from $.35 to $.45 an hour. Also, you'll be given two free passes each week you can give to anybody you want." The big increase in pay was enough for me to agree immediately to accept the exalted position.

In retrospect, I should have listened more carefully to the responsibilities of a head usher. The pay increase and the free passes were great but the increased work load was pretty heavy.

I had to start coming in on Saturday mornings and pop enough popcorn to last a full week. The popcorn popper was a huge machine, located on the second floor behind the movie screen. The popcorn was put into ten gallon tins which had to be carried down the stairs, through the movie auditorium, out into the lobby, and then downstairs to the basement where they were stored until needed up at the snack counter. That process every Saturday morning took a long time.

Each time the movie was changed, Mr. Grist would write out the words he wanted to go on the outside marquee that would, in his mind, make the movie irresistible to passers-by. This change was made during the last movie shown that evening.

I went down into the basement and pulled the correct letters and numbers from the shelves where they were stored. The numbers and letters were made of heavy black plastic about five inches high. The outside marquee had two sides that projected over the sidewalk so I had to pull two of everything. By the time all the numbers and letters were pulled and put into boxes for carrying outside, the boxes would be fairly heavy.

I had to get a tall step-ladder from the basement to stand on while I removed the old word letters and hang the new word letters. Each time I hung the new letters I had to climb down the letter, step back some distance, and view my handiwork. Spacing was very important. After I finished, Mr. Grist or his assistant, Mr. Potts, would come out and approve my work or make me climb back up and make some adjustments.

"Hey, Kenan, you left out the "e" in the word "HERE," Mr. Potts would say. Sure enough when I looked up at the marquee the words were "FROM HER TO ETERNITY."

I looked at the words that Mr. Grist had given me and showed Mr. Potts I had put the letters the way Mr. Grist had written them. I had to go back down into the basement, get two more "E"s, climb up the ladder on each side of the marquee and put the "E" in its proper place.

One other responsibility of a head usher was to distribute some movie posters in the downtown area. This was done in the afternoon on the final day the current movie was showing. I had to put a poster in the lobbies of the Hotel Wilmington and the Brunswick Hotel, which were located on North Front Street. Hotel Wilmington was often referred to as the "Bugg Hotel" because it was owned by Mr. E. B. Bugg.

56   HOTELS

HOTEL WILMINGTON

Modern Fireproof Hotel

RATE
$2.75 to $4.00
PER DAY

Storage Garage

E. B. BUGG
Owner and Operator   TELS. 7711-7712-7713

I dreaded going into the lobby in the Brunswick Hotel on the northwest corner of Front and Grace Streets. The hotel guests that hung about in the lobby were not the kind of people that stayed in the Cape Fear Hotel or Hotel Wilmington. I felt they were staring at me and planning on taking my two free passes to the Bailey Theatre.

Another responsibility of the head usher was to carry the film canisters after the final showing of a movie down to the Bijou Theatre where the movie rental company came by to pick up the canisters. The film for a move was on two large reels. Each theatre had a projector room, located at the rear of the theatre. Inside were two large projectors into which the two movie reels were placed.

The projectionist, at the proper time, would start the first projector. As the film in that projector neared the end, a bell would ding to alert the projectionist the reel was almost finished, and a few seconds later, a dark circle would show up on the screen. At that instant, the projectionist was supposed to turn on the second projector. If the projectionist was skilled, the audience wouldn't even notice the change-over. If the projectionist wasn't skilled, he may turn on the second projector early or late. Sometimes, the second projector wouldn't even run. These kinds of interruptions displeased the audience greatly and cries of "Bijou, Bijou" would be heard.

I had to lug the two heavy canisters up Front Street to the Bijou, the sister theatre of the Bailey. This was usually done around 11 or 11:30 at night. After delivering the canisters, I had to walk home by myself to 408 Church Street. In those days, I had no worries anyone would bother me as I walked the ten blocks home, and no one ever did.

As always whenever I landed a job, I gave some thought as to whether I could make a career at that business. While working at the Bailey, on nights when the movie was showing for the last time, I would go up into the projection room and wait for the movie to end. The projectionist, Mr. Thigpen, would rewind the reels of film and put them into canisters for me to lug down to the Bijou for pickup by the film distributor.

During the summer of 1952, while I was staying with Mr. Jim Futreal's family and putting in tobacco, his son, Toogie, was the projectionist at the Hula Drive-in Theatre. If I couldn't find any girls in the Chicken House with whom to have an interesting conversation, I would walk into the projection building and spend some time with Toogie. Toogie was younger than I was and I often wondered how hard it could be to operate movie projectors.

I told Mr. Thigpen about my experiences in the projection room at the Hula. Impressed with my knowledge of the intricacies of projection of movies, he would sometimes permit me to switch from the projector that was showing the film to the second projector when the time was right for switching.

One evening during the last showing of *Singing in the Rain,* Mr. Thigpen had to make an emergency visit to the restroom and left me in charge to make the last switchover. I became distracted somewhat. Although I heard the bell indicating switching time was near, I looked away for an instant. When I looked back at the screen, I thought I saw the dark circle so I started the second projector. It was a few seconds too early. There were double images of Gene Kelly, Debby Reynolds and Donald O'Connor singing and dancing in the rain while one sound track was playing *"Fit as a Fiddle"* and the other was playing *"Make 'em Laugh."*

Mr. Grist called up the projection booth to inquire what the "H..." was going on. I tried to sound like Mr. Thigpen when I answered. "Yes, sir, the bell went off a little early for some reason I can't figure out. First time that's ever happened that I can remember. Maybe all that rain caused a shortage. Ha, Ha."

Mr. Grist wasn't amused. "See that it doesn't happen again or I may be looking for a new projectionist."

When Mr. Thigpen returned, I decided not to say anything to him about the possibility of his having to look for another job. After that, I tried to stay clear of the projection room.

Before that night, I had considered a career in the theatre business; perhaps as a manager or better yet, a projectionist. All he did was sit around for four or five hours and turn switches on and off four or five times and for that, he got paid a dollar an hour. That event caused me to look some more for my lifetime vocation.

"Bwana Devil," the first 3-D movie, was shown at the Baily. People were lined all the way to Market Street on the day of the first showing. Everyone was anxious to see a 3-D movie. As head usher, I had the responsibility of standing outside at the ticket booth, in my official usher outfit, and handing each ticket purchaser a pair of 3-D glasses. It was a strange sight to see the theatre completely full, including the balconies, with everyone sitting there expectantly with what looked like a pair of sunglasses on.

It was exciting to see a spear coming out of the screen right into your face, or see a lion jump right into your lap. Unfortunately, the movie itself wasn't all that good. Robert Stack and Barbara Britton didn't put in Oscar winning performances. After the movie, the streets were littered with discarded 3-D glasses although a few patrons took their glasses home for use at the next 3-D movie in the implausible event a second one would be made.

Another responsibility for the head usher was to periodically man the snack counter in the balcony reserved for blacks. From this location, you had a panoramic view of the entire theatre, including the back row of the balcony used by white customers.

At times during my career at the Bailey, I saw some dating couples, some of whom were in my classes, having interesting conversations on the back row. That kind of behavior would not have been tolerated at the Hula Drive-in Theatre in Chinquapin. Delmas Cottle, the Chicken House Monitor, with his huge flashlight, would have put them in the spotlight with a warning: "Cut that out right now or I'll tell your parents."

The Bailey Theatre ordinarily scheduled only the top hit movies. One of the better attended movies, "Ivanhoe," was adapted from the famous novel by Sir Walter Scott. It starred Robert Taylor, Elizabeth Taylor, George Sanders, and Joan Fontaine. Robert Taylor was the hero who tried to help Richard the Lionhearted regain his throne following his disastrous journey on The Third Crusade. Even Robin Hood and his Merry Men had a part to play in the movie.

Miss Frances Formyduval recommended her English Literature students go see the film. Apparently, many of her students took her advice. In her column "Teen-Age Tattler," reporter Sherry Rich wrote the following report:

"Some of the folks seen enjoying the picture were: Louise Saunders, Kenneth Alexander, Charles Hicks, Holmes Davis, Mutt Saunders, Bob Godley, Ernest Anderson, Miriam Hickman, Betty Smithson, Catherine Herring and David Barefoot. The teachers seemed to have a special liking for this movie, too. Also sighted at one of the showings were Mr. and Mrs. Hayward Bellamy and Mr. and Mrs. T. P. Brown."

On Halloween night, Friday, October 31, 1952, Mr. Grist had scheduled a special showing of a horror movie, "The Black Castle," starring Boris Karloff. The movie took place on the Austrian estate of Count Von Bruno.

The theatre was full that night, mostly of NHHS students. Earlier they had seen the Wildcats defeat the Wilson Cyclones 27-12 before a crowd of 5,800 fans. Sonny Jurgensen didn't have one of his better passing nights, just eight completions out of seventeen attempts.

One of those completions was a 15 yarder to George Gaddy for a touchdown. George had to punt only three times during the game but had a forty-four yard average on his punts.

The NHHS Students had gone to the Community Center after the game for the usual Friday night dance and then decided to go to the Bailey for the horror movie. They were all keyed up and some of them were very active. Flattened popcorn boxes were flying everywhere. As head usher, I tried to maintain a decent level of noise but I failed. If I only had Miss Walsh or Mrs. Josie Brock, two very strict teachers at NHHS, with me, I think they could have restored decorum quickly.

At the conclusion of the movie, Mr. Grist had arranged to cut off all the lights and a couple of men he had hired to run up and down the aisles screaming at the top of their voices. Their faces were painted with luminous paint to make them look like zombies.

Things didn't go as planned. Several girls in the audience panicked, started screaming and running for the exits. Some of the boys on the football team began running up and down the aisles, in the dark, yelling their heads off. Others followed them.

The two zombies were almost trampled to death in the melee. Some of the football players were rather small but several of them were rather large. The zombies had no protective gear. Mr. Grist had to pay them an extra five dollars each to compensate them for their injuries. He never tried anything like that again.

Unbeknownst to me, one of the young ladies who worked at the candy counter was the older sister of my future wife. Barbara Maultsby came to work at the Bailey immediately after graduating from Acme-Delco High School.

Chapter 20
My Junior Year Begins

Some of the courses I took in the school year 1952-1953 were: U. S. History under Mrs. Josie Brock, Biology under Coach Bill Brooks, and French 1 under Mr. Thomas Brown. I had been so inspired seeing the ROTC units marching in the

Azalea Parade earlier that year, I signed up to take ROTC. I was assigned to Company D under Cadet Captain Paul Burton. The Company D Sponsor that year was Jane Love, the girl who had made me feel welcome to NHHS on my first day there in January, 1951.

Other ROTC units were Company A under Cadet Lt. Harry Stone, Mary Catherine White, Sponsor: Company B under Cadet Captain Bruce Ludlum, Lucille Barden, Sponsor; Company C under Cadet Captain Ed Caldwell, Sue Edwards, Sponsor.

Although I took ROTC for two years, it wasn't as beneficial as I had hoped. However, I did learn some basic skills such as marching and taking an M-1 rifle apart and putting it back together again. These skills came in handy later when I served in the National Guard and the Air Force.

We had to wear our ROTC uniforms twice weekly, on Mondays and Fridays. On those mornings all units would march to the 13th and Ann Field with the ROTC band playing. I had two problems with my uniform. I could never get my brass polished good enough and I had never worn a tie before and didn't know how to tie a good military knot.

Johnny Hinnant said to me one day in study hall, "Kenan, do you know, I think you've got the worst looking knot I've ever seen. Don't you know how to tie a tie? Do you want me to show you how I tie my tie?"

I really did need some help so I accepted his offer. "Well, the first thing you do is to draw your right knee up to your chest and wrap the tie around your knee as if it was your neck with the big end of the tie in your hand. Then you push that end of the tie through the loop, wrap it around the small end, pull it back through the loop and then pull it through the loop at the front of the tie that you just made. Understand?"

I had no idea what he had just said. "I thought you were supposed to be a quick learner with a photographic memory," he said. "Here, I'll show you. Take off your tie."

"Wait a minute. If I take off my tie and can't get it back on they'll get me at my ROTC class," I said.

"Don't worry. I guarantee when I get finished you'll have the best looking tie in Company D with the possible exception of Pete Land." [8]

I took my tie off and he proceeded to demonstrate his tie-tying technique on his own knee. After he had demonstrated the technique a few times, I tried it and it worked. I ended up with a beautiful Windsor knot. All I had to do was then put the tie around my neck, under the collar, and pull it tight. After that learning experience, I only had to worry about getting my brass polished to a satisfactory gloss.

Life was going on pretty much as usual at NHHS until on October 26, 1952, there was a terrible accident on North Lumina Avenue at Wrightsville Beach in which one of our classmates, David Camak, lost his life. He had been riding with some of his friends on Lumina Avenue and either fell or jumped from the moving car. He died later at James Walker Memorial Hospital.

Some NHHS students had been unfortunate enough to have to spend some time in the hospital but this event was so traumatic, everyone was in a state of shock. Just that fall, Rex Hardy had spent some time in the hospital as the result of a football accident. Jack Watson had spent some time in the hospital also the result of a football accident, and Joanne Blackburn had spent some time in the hospital for a surgical procedure. But to think that David wasn't coming back from his accident was traumatic.

The month of November, 1952 was a very busy time for NHHS students, not only with respect to sports but also with respect to political and intellectual matters.

We were particularly interested in the presidential election that took place in November. The Democratic candidate was Adlai Stevenson and the Republican Candidate was General Dwight Eisenhower. At the last assembly prior to the date of election, there were speeches made by students for the two candidates.

Speaking for Mr. Stevenson were Channey Grant, Sylvia Wilson, Grant Armstrong, and Joe Tardugno. Speaking for

---

[8] Pete Land was an excellent student and won many honors in the ROTC program at NHHS.

General Eisenhower were Ashton Godley, Janie Valentine and Mary Catherine Cole. Each speech was followed by a rousing march played by Catherine von der Leith, Charles Snipes, Robert Cole, Bill Sparkes, Daffney Lewis, Robert Ellis, Jack Smith, and Emerson Head.

My father and my grandfather had been staunch Republicans all their lives. They were always very badly outnumbered in Chinquapin by the "Yellow Dog Democrats." I followed in their footsteps in my political beliefs and shook my head in sorrow when I heard the Democratic supporters speak, especially Joe Tardugno. He was a very good friend and played on our basketball team, the Wolverines. I didn't understand how such an intelligent person could support the Democratic Party.

Fortunately, in my view, General Eisenhower won the general election and was elected the 34th President of the United States. The voters in New Hanover County didn't agree with me or the rest of the country. Mr. Stevenson received 10,245 votes as compared with 9,267 for General Eisenhower. Voters in the city of Wilmington voted even more heavily for Mr. Stevenson; 7,322 for him and 5,824 for General Eisenhower.

The NHHS Wildcats didn't have a winning season even though Sonny Jurgensen was selected as the quarterback for the All-State Football Team for 1952. The team lost its final game to the Fayetteville Bulldogs, 7 – 0, before 5,000 fans in Fayetteville.

Sonny Jurgensen played all three major sports at NHHS. Although football seemed to be his favorite sport, he was also very good at basketball and baseball. He also enjoyed playing tricks on people.

One rainy day in December, when the school went on a "Rainy Day" schedule with dancing in the gym and movies in the auditorium, Sonny and some of his basketball team mates were having a free-shooting contest in the gym. There was usually more pick-up basketball played than dancing.

Sonny was on the foul line where he had just made seven straight free throws. Just as he got ready to shoot his eighth shot, Mr. Arwood, the PE teacher walked by almost under the goal. He had a drink in his hand which he had just purchased from the vending machine in a little room off the court. Sonny took careful aim and let the shot go. It was a perfect shot, missing the backboard completely and hitting Mr. Arwood's hand just as he was taking a sip. The orange drink splattered over his face and his shirt.

Mr. Arwood was enraged. "Jurgensen, you did that on purpose," he yelled as he wiped his face with his handkerchief. "You're a better shot than that. Didn't he do that on purpose, boys?" He appealed to Sonny's teammates. They remained silent.

"No, sir, Mr. Arwood," Sonny vehemently protested. Sometimes people just make bad shots. The ball slips out of your hands. That happens to me a lot when I'm trying to pass a football. It was a mistake."

Mr. Arwood walked on to his office still complaining under his breath. As soon as he disappeared from view, Sonny and his teammates burst into laughter.

I usually went into the gym during the "Rainy Day" schedule. I had tried the movies in the auditorium a few times but whoever selected the movies to be shown had very bad judgment. Many times cartoons were shown, more appropriate for kindergartners than high school students. The favorite was *"Steamboat Willie,"* the forerunner of Mickey Mouse.

Rather than dance, some of my friends and I would play a pick-up basketball game. As it could get very warm in the gym, after thirty minutes of brisk playing, some of the boys would be perspiring heavily. We would have to go back to our classes without showering or changing clothes. Some teachers and even some students, mostly girls, objected to being exposed to the unpleasant odors.

Chapter 21
We Move Again

In early December, 1952, we moved again. This time it was a very short move, from 408 to 407 Church Street, directly across the street. The apartment in 408 Church was very nice but a little more expensive than we could afford. The house at 407 Church was small and not in very good shape. It was located directly behind the Christian Advent Church which stood on the northeast corner of Fourth and Church Streets.

This move was the only time Mother didn't use Williams Moving Company. We simply moved ourselves. Joan, Gerald and I enlisted some of our Dry Pond friends to help us move. We would pick up an item and carry it across the street to our new home and then walk back across the street and repeat the process.

At times during the day, I saw Miss. Brady looking out of her upstairs living room window. We must have reminded her of a colony of ants as they carry food to their nest and then went back to get more.

Several ushers at the Bailey Theatre lived on Fourth Street or nearby: Winston Thompson, Floyd Gore, Eddie Kraus, and Bobby Britt. A classmate of mine, Sally Yopp, lived at 307 Church Street. Her father was a salesman at Raney Chevrolet Company. A 1939 graduate of NHHS, "Tanky" Meier and his family lived at 412 Church St. Tanky was an outstanding tennis player at NHHS while a student there.

Dry Pond was a nice community, a mixture of residences, single family and apartments, and small businesses. The most popular place for teen-agers was Drake's Bakery on the northwest corner of Fourth and Castle Streets. The store was divided into two sections: a café that sold hot dogs, hamburgers, sodas, etc. with a juke box and booths on the right side while the left side contained the bakery.

Drake's Bakery

It was the place to hang-out for the teenagers who lived in Dry Pond. The juke box was kept busy while the kids danced. No matter when you went, there always seemed to be some of your friends eating, talking or dancing. In some ways, going to Drake's was similar to "cruisin' around the Chic-Chic Grill, or the Miljo, except we were walking rather than driving.

There were several small corner grocery stores in the neighborhood. Our favorite was Joe's Grocery owned and operated by Mr. Joe Rouse. It was located on the southwest corner of Fourth and Nun Streets. Mr. Rouse would permit Mother to charge some purchases if she didn't have the money at that time of the month. When the allotment check from the Navy came at the beginning of the month, she would walk over to Joe's and settle up.

My friend, Leonard, had a part-time job at one of those Dry Pond grocery stores, Mills Grocery, on the corner of Third and Castle Streets. He asked me to work for him one weekend as he had to go out of town. I hesitated because I was rather busy as the Baily. But as Mr. Mills closed his store at 6 PM and I didn't have to report to the Baily until 6:30 PM, I agreed to help Leonard.

Mill's Superette

Mr. Mills wasn't very pleasant person as I soon found out, at least not to his hired help. My job was to work in the stockroom, keep the counters and display shelves filled with merchandise, and deliver groceries to customers who lived within walking distance. Most of my deliveries were to the Cape Fear Apartments, just up the street. One of my classmates, Tommy Cook and his family, lived there.

It was hard work. Mr. Mills didn't want to see me taking any kind of rest break. Near closing time, he told me to go to the stock room and clean up. As I was cleaning up, I spotted a basket of lettuce which, to my way of thinking, looked very old, wilted, and discolored. I took the basket out back and threw the lettuce into the trash bin.

Mr. Mills came in a few minutes later and couldn't find his lettuce. He asked me and I had to confess I had tossed it away in accordance with his orders to clean up the stockroom.

"You what?" He shouted. "Why'd you do that?"

"Mr. Mills," I said. "You wouldn't try to sell that lettuce to your customers, would you? Go outside and take a look at it. It really doesn't look like the Health Department would give it a passing grade."

"Why, there wasn't anything wrong with that lettuce. It could be fluffed up, turned upside down, exposed to fresh air and it would good as new. Don't you have any sense? I'm going to take a dollar out of your pay."

As my pay was only four dollars for the day, that left me with three dollars. I was glad to get out of there with that much. If I had worked there much longer, I believe I would have ended up owing Mr. Mills some money.

Leonard seemed to be satisfied working his way up in the grocery store business. He had aspirations of being the manager of an A & P store one day. Early on the morning I checked in at Mills Superette, I was thinking perhaps a career as a grocery store manager at the A & P or at Patricia's Super Market wouldn't be bad. However, the day's experience at Mills convinced me I didn't have a future in the grocery store business.

Mr. George Carroll and his family lived at 404 Church Street. Mr. Carroll was a pharmacist at Lane's Drug Store on the southwest corner of Sixteenth and Market Streets. He had two daughters and a very young son. The two daughters, Elaine and Linda, were a little younger than me. If someone in my family was sick and Mother couldn't afford to take us to the doctor or to buy the required medication, Mr. Carroll would do his best to help take care of our medical problems.

Halloween in Dry Pond[9] was an exciting time. The streets were full of kids running around, ringing doorbells, fighting with other kids about various and sundry things. It was chaos. The adults didn't seem to mind. They just kept calmly handing out treats as the kids came by and exclaiming about how wonderful the costumes were.

Chapter 22
Sunday School at Catherine Kennedy Home

Miss Cornelia Brady, who now lived across the street from us, kept up with my church attendance. If she saw me out on the street when she returned from church on Sundays, she would call me over and chastise me for skipping Sunday services. She knew my Sunday School teacher, Mr. Daniel Todd, who had also been my English teacher in the ninth grade. Miss Brady's goal was to make me a Sunday School teacher one day. She asked Mr. Todd to let me help him teach his class sometimes. I didn't mind that too badly as I knew I needed to overcome my shyness, especially when it came to speaking to a group.

Miss Brady was also very interested in the Catherine Kennedy Home, a home for elderly ladies on the southeastern corner of Third and Orange Streets, just across from the First Presbyterian Church. On the fourth Sunday of the month, a member of First Baptist Church would conduct a shortened worship service in the small chapel at the Home.

One evening Miss Brady saw me out in the street, playing football with Gerald and Coleman. She came over and told me that the Deacon who was scheduled to conduct the worship service at the Catherine Kennedy Home the next Sunday had to go out of town unexpectedly. She asked me if I would consider conducting the service. I was very reluctant. She explained the old ladies didn't expect very much; just sing one

---

[9] There was once a pond in this section which eventually dried up. The exact location of the pond is unknown.

or two hymns, a short devotional that could be read, and a closing prayer.

I wanted to please Miss Brady because she was always so nice to me and my family, I finally agreed. I spent the next few evenings writing down what I planned to say. I tried to memorize it but finally gave up on that idea. I didn't think I would be able to carry that off before a group of people.

I had planned to arrive about 9:25 AM, five minutes before the scheduled starting time but I had trouble tying my tie of all mornings.

. When I walked into the little sanctuary at 9:28 AM, the group was already singing the opening hymn, "How Great Thou Art." Or I should say one lady was singing and the others were making some quiet noises. I went up to the front, picked up a hymnal and tried to find the correct page, but as it turned out there were three different hymnals in the pews and the one I selected didn't have "How Great Thou Art."

Meanwhile, the pianist and the one singer were struggling bravely but with very little support. The pianist encouraged them; "Then sings my soul.....Some of the rest of you sing, for God's sake...How great thou art, How great thou art..." I never could find the song in my hymnal so all I could do was nod my head and hum.

After the song had mercifully ended, I stood up to introduce myself. Meanwhile, several latecomers had arrived, one lady using a walker with a seat ingeniously built in so that she could sit down whenever she felt the need. Unfortunately, another lady who had arrived earlier, also with a walker, had left her walker in the aisle so that other "walkered" people couldn't get by.

Wanting to be helpful, I went to move the walker out of the way but the owner protested loudly. "Don't take my walker, I can't walk without it." I tried to explain I only wanted to move it for a second but she didn't want it moved under any circumstances and wouldn't give in graciously to any sort of movement.

Meanwhile, the other lady had sat down on her walker in the middle of the aisle, apparently prepared to sit there during the worship service. However, the seat was attached to the backside of the walker so she was sitting with her back to the front of the room. I was finally able to find a seat for her and get her out of the aisle, facing me, in the proper church worship position.

I started my "sermon," but some of the attendees spoke up saying they couldn't hear me. I had forgotten to turn on the P.A. system. I reached over to turn it on, not knowing the previous user had turned up the volume to the highest level for some unknown reason. When it came on, the sound almost knocked the socks off the entire congregation. All the old ladies screamed and covered their ears.

I had a very good lesson about the importance of persistent prayer (which I personally put to good use at the time). After the service was over, I stood at the rear of the chapel, speaking to the people as they departed. One lady, as she shook my hand, secretively left a Kleenex wrapped around a one dollar bill.

1952 Top Songs, Movies and Books

Top Ten Songs
  Blue Tango by Leroy Anderson
  Wheel of Fortune by Kay Starr
  Cry by Johnnie Ray
  You Belong to Me by Joe Stafford
  Auf Wiedersch'n Sweetheart by Vera Lynn
  Half as Much by Rosemary Clooney
  Wish You Were Here by Eddie Fisher
  I Went To Your Wedding by Patti Page
  Here in My Heart by Al Martino
  Delicado by Percy Faith

Top Five Movies
  The Greatest Show on Earth with Betty Hutton,
    Charleston Heston, Cornel Wilde, Gloria Grahame
  The Bad and the Beautiful with Lana Turner, Kirk Douglas
  The Snows of Kilimanjaro with Gregory Peck, Ava Gardner
  Singin' In the Rain with Gene Kelly, Debbie Reynolds
  Ivanhoe with Robert Taylor, Elizabeth Taylor

Top Five Books
The Silver Chalice by Thomas Costain
East of Eden by John Steinbeck
My Cousin Rachel by Daphne Du Maurier
Steamboat Gothic by Frances Parkinson Keyes
Giant by Edna Ferber

Chapter 23
Back to School – Spring of 1953

After the Christmas holiday were over, students were "eager" to get back to school. Or they would have been except that they were faced almost immediately with the prospect of mid-term exams. Most of us had forgotten everything we had learned during the holidays. Everywhere you looked you would see students cramming for the exams or at least talking about how hard they were cramming.

After mid-term exams were completed and students who had done well had finished sharing their good news and students who hadn't done so well shared their bad news, academic life, social life, and athletic life resumed in full force.

I had two good friends, Grier White and Billy Wall, who were now on the swimming team. Grier asked me to try out for the team but I didn't feel I had the time. Besides carrying a heavy academic load at NHHS, I was working several hours a week at the Bailey Theater and playing basketball for the Wolverines in the City League two or three times a week.

In order to show me where the Aquacats swam, they took me to an aqua show in March, 1953, at the YMCA pool. The YMCA, located at the corner of Third and Market Streets, didn't have a world-class pool. It was in the basement, had only six lanes, and the length of the pool was only twenty-five yards. In the swimming contests, contestants had to do a lot of turns, especially in the 200 yard events. Another sort of unusual feature of the YMCA pool was that, except for meets and other public events, male swimmers were not allowed to wear swimwear.

In the Aqua Show there were colorful events scheduled including the balloon figure, water wheel by eight mermaids, mass dolphin dives and the finale was all swimmers holding candles in the blacked-out room.

Several interesting demonstrations were held. These included an exhibition of the backstroke by Don Frost, the breaststroke by Oscar Grant, free style by George Lewis, and fancy diving by Grier White, Barbara Batson, Roxana Mebane and Dianne Snakenburg. And then Ann Key, Oscar Grant, Don Frost, Eric Oertel, and Sue Walker gave a life-saving demonstration.

The most interesting event was the eating of a banana by Ed Dye while underwater. All in all, it was a very successful show.

Swimming in the YMCA pool was quite different from swimming in Halso Swamp although we never wore swim trunks there either.

Although I wasn't personally responsible for ROTC Cadet Captain Paul Burton being selected as the fourth recipient of the "Cape Fear Sword," an award presented annually to an outstanding cadet officer by the SENC Citadel Alumni club, I was in his company, Company D. The award reflected well on all the ROTC cadets in Paul's company.

The citation read as follows: "…..*the annual award of the Cape Fear Sword is made to that member of the Junior ROTC who possesses the finest character, outstanding qualities of leadership, military proficiency, and participation in extra-curricular activities.* Paul told a reporter he is a "career soldier" and plans to enter the Citadel after graduation from high school.

The team I was on in the City League was a fairly good team. The quality of play certainly wasn't as good as in high school games but there were some good players in the league. In our final game that spring, Coach Leon Brogden came to the Community Center to watch some games. Just by chance, I scored 30 points in that game.

After the game, Coach Brogden came up to me and said," you played a pretty good game out there tonight. Did you ever think about trying out for the school team?"

I could hardly believe Coach Brogden thought I played well enough to try out for the Wildcats. "No, sir," I said. "I thought I was good enough to make the team at Chinquapin but not here. There're too many real good players."

There was some truth to my reason for not trying out but the real reason was I needed to work to earn money to help with family needs.

Trying out for the Wildcat basketball team would have required a lot of time and if, by some chance, I made the team, afternoon practices, evening games, and especially out-of-town games, made my participation impossible. [10]

When school let out on Monday afternoon, March 9, 1953, everyone's eyes were directed towards downtown Wilmington. Huge clouds of black smoke were billowing up from that direction all day. We could hear fire truck sirens coming from every direction and all were headed towards downtown. We learned from Mr. Capps a warehouse down on the river was on fire.

We couldn't let an opportunity to see a big fire pass us by so my Dry Pond friends and I walked downtown from the school instead of going home. The closer we got to the waterfront, the worse the fire and smoke appeared. We got within a block of the fire but weren't allowed to get any closer by the police for our own safety they said.

We sat down on a hill in the area of Second and Harnett Streets to enjoy the spectacle. We had been there a few minutes when I saw someone who looked like my friend, Sammy Hill, approach the police who waved him inside the safety perimeter.

"Look," I said. "There's Sammy Hill being let in to get closer to the fire. How come they let him in? Just because he's set on being a fireman he must have some pull with the fire department."

---

[10]   After coming back to Wilmington in 1964, and attending services at First Baptist Church regularly, I became good friends with Coach Brogden. I later taught the Sunday School class of which he was a member. He was one of the most modest men I ever knew and a true Southern gentleman. His wife, Mrs. Sally Brogden, was as gracious and unassuming as anyone could be. She was a true Southern lady.

I stood up and yelled out, "Hey, Sammy, how come you get to be closer? Can you help me get in?"

He turned and I saw right away it wasn't Sammy Hill but a middle-aged man with a badge of some kind on his shirt. I quietly sat back down and said to my friends, "If that had been Sammy, he would have got me in, I think."

We learned later the fire was the largest in Wilmington's history. It had started in one of the warehouses from defective wiring. Seeing the fireboat "Annie" spraying water on the fire as well as the occasional explosions was better than watching "*Bwana Devil*".

Eighteen firemen and civilians were injured but thankfully no one was killed. The fire did an estimated three million dollars in damage. Finally, the firemen got the fire under control and we walked back to Dry Pond. Smoke from the fire hung over the town, even over Dry Pond.

After the excitement over the waterfront fire was passed, I turned my attention to more serious things. The Wilmington Star-News conducted a survey in March, 1953, to determine the favorite comic strip. I was an avid reader of "*The Phantom, The Ghost Who Walks,*" and urged everyone I knew to vote for the masked crusader. I never stopped to wonder why I was such a fan of a man who wore gray tights and a mask and lived in the jungle.

I believe his oath to defend the innocent may have influenced me in my admiration: *"I swear to devote my life to the destruction of piracy, greed, cruelty and injustice. And my sons and their sons shall follow me."* The fact his sons and grandsons followed him explained how the Phantom never seemed to die.

Anyway, I was gratified to learn *"The Phantom"* came in first followed by *"Boots and her Buddies," "Little Orphan Annie," "Gasoline Alley," "Captain Easy," "Rip Kirby," "Abbie and Slats," "Jane Arden,"* and *"Terry and the Pirates."*

The survey wasn't as enjoyable as the fire had been but nonetheless, it confirmed my belief "The Phantom" was the best comic strip at the time.

The NHHS tennis team wasn't having a particularly good season in the spring of 1953. On May 13, 1953, they defeated Kinston 9-0 for their third victory against six losses. Buddy Davis, Gary Preston, Greg Davis, Pete Land, Bob Coleman, and Gene Johnson all won their singles matches. In the doubles matches, Buddy Davis and Greg Davis won, as did Gary Preston and Gene Johnson.

However, the NHHS Golf Team was doing pretty good. On March 10, 1953, they beat the Whiteville team 16-2 for their sixth win of the season. Playing for NHHS were Freddie Butters, Alex Efird, Gatchell Joye and David Sloan. Johnny Covington wasn't able to play in this match.

Another NHHS student, Donald Graziano, was honored by receiving the Teen-Age award, presented by the Benevolent Fund of the Wilmington Police Department. Donald was president of the student body, a major in ROTC, a member of the NHHS Handbook Staff and was amateur flyweight boxing champion of eastern North Carolina. He won the Golden Gloves flyweight championship eight times in ten years.

I kind of felt ashamed of myself. During the entire year, I hadn't done anything worthy of being honored or given an award. I pledged to try and do better next year.

Chapter 24
Azalea Festival 1953

As always, the Annual Azalea Festival was the biggest event of the year for Wilmington and New Hanover County. Many prominent citizens served on the various committees that were necessary to ensure that every detail of the Festival was well planned. I didn't have a very big role, only marching with ROTC Company D in the parade.

Planning for the next festival began almost immediately after one ended. On February 11, 1953, there was a pre-Azalea Festival dance at the Moose Temple featuring Tex Beneke and his 18 piece band. The dance was attended by nearly 800 people and one-half hour of the dance was broadcast live nationwide over the Mutual Broadcasting System. Lou Essick, disc jockey for the 1340 Club on WGNI radio, served as master of ceremonies.

Selecting the Queen for the Azalea Festival was a very important part of the Festival. Movie stars were the queens of choice. In 1953, the Azalea Festival Committee announced that somebody named Ursula Thiess would be the queen.

At that time, Miss Thiess had been in a few movies and was called "the most beautiful woman in the world," For some reason, never publicly explained, Miss Thiess was replaced by Alexis Smith as the Azalea Queen.

Jerry Barber won the Azalea Open Golf Tournament in 1953 with a winning purse of $2,000.00.

To the great surprise of the public, a lengthy report appeared in the April 1, 1953, issue of the Wilmington Star News concerning a heated controversy between three of the County Commissioners and the Wilmington Azalea Festival Committee. The controversy arose over the planned erection of bleacher reviewing stands along the sidewalk in front of the courthouse. The City of Wilmington had given permission to the Committee to contract with a firm to erect the stands.

Just as the contractor was about to begin construction of the stands, he was confronted by the County Attorney, Mr. Marsden Bellamy, who intimated he would be arrested if he proceeded with the construction. Apparently, this action was taken under the direction of County Commissioners Ralph Horton, Raiford Trask and Thurston Watkins.

The President of the Azalea Festival Committee, Mr. Rye B. Page, Jr., wrote a lengthy report about his discussions with the Commissioners which reads in part as follows:

"Upon entering the office I observed the three commissioners sitting about. I addressed my remarks to Chairman Horton and asked him what the trouble was. He said that they had not been informed about the bleachers and objected to their being placed in front of the courthouse. I explained they had not been informed because I thought that all that was necessary was permission of the City."

"I explained that this permission had been granted. Mr. Horton then said that they had promised seats in the offices to people and that now they would be unable to see. I repeated Mr. Benson's offer of free tickets and told him to give me a list and we would be glad that each person would receive a free ticket."

"He did not accept or decline this offer but launched into the subject of having spent a lot of money to clean and decorate the courthouse so it would look nice for the Festival weekend. I asked him if the money was spent on the cleaning and repairing just for the parade or if it had been done because it needed it."

"Mr. O'shields spoke up and said that the work was voted for because there was a definite need for it. This was the only time Mr. O'shields spoke. The rest of the time the other commissioners present did the talking. Another objection was that we would block the door and disrupt the traffic that would be going to court. I pointed out that the stands would be split in front of the steps providing a five foot path to the steps and that there were two other entrances on Princess Street to take care of people who had to use the courthouse."

"I left their office and went and talked with Mr. Robbins, the contractor, who intimated he was going to take his bleachers and return to Gastonia. I persuaded him to go back into the Commissioners' office and talk to them with me. He consented to do this but said it would do no good. When we returned to the office, I repeated what he had said to me to the group and asked if it were true. I was told that Mr. Robbins

had been told not to erect bleachers past a certain point, but that Robbins had not been threatened with arrest. I asked Robbins had he been told that he would be arrested and he said he had not."

"It was then that the County Attorney, Marsden Bellamy, spoke up and said that he had asked Robbins his name in case a warrant was necessary and that he had called in Sheriff Register and Solicitor John Walker because he felt they might be needed. It was Mr. Walker who gave the interpretation of the City ordinance concerning blocking the sidewalks and stated that his job was to see that a person brought into court was duly tried and other than that he had nothing to do with the case."

"After all this had taken place, I asked Mr. Robbins if he would erect the bleachers on another spot if one could be found and he then said that he had been scared out and he was taking down the stands that had been erected and returning to Gastonia but he still wanted his guarantee of $500."

""After leaving the office of the Commissioners, I called our treasurer, Mr. Broadfoot, and asked that he bring me a check in the amount of $500 for Mr. Robbins with our apologies for an embarrassing and unfortunate incident."

On April 2, 1953, the Azalea Festival Committee unanimously accepted Mr. Page's report and gave him a standing vote of thanks with great applause. There followed some discussion about taking some action against the three commissioners because of the loss of revenue by not having the bleachers. Mr. Hugh Morton stated that the loss was certainly more than $100 and may have been as much as $400. The Committee decided not to take any action."

Who knew such a raging controversy was going on behind the scenes about such an innocuous project? The community's leading citizens aired their dirty linen in public.

Despite this incident, the 1953 Azalea Festival was hailed as a great success if only more bleacher seats had been available.

Also held in 1953 in connection with the Azalea Festival was the first annual Azalea Festival Harness Race at Legion Stadium. Numerous harness racing horses were housed in the stable barn adjacent to Legion Stadium year around. A total of nineteen horses from seven states participated in the race.

Harness Racing at Legion Stadium

Chapter 25
The Death of Eddie Kraus

On the evening of Tuesday, July 14, 1953, we heard some sirens approaching Dry Pond. They became so loud I ran outside to see what was happening. I saw some police cars coming up Church Street from the direction of Third Street and then make a right turn onto Fourth Street. Gerald, Coleman, and I ran over to Fourth Street and saw the police cars had stopped in front of Eddie Kraus' house at 516 South Fourth Street.

By this time, several other people had come out of their homes and were walking towards Eddie's house. Just as we approached the house, an ambulance came roaring up. A couple of medical technicians rushed into the house with a stretcher. They were inside only a few minutes when we saw them come out with a body on the stretcher. It was put into the ambulance which took off at a high rate of speed with its sirens wailing.

Everyone was talking and questioning others trying to learn what had happened. Word began to spread that someone in the house had been shot. As it was Eddie's house, I wondered if he had been shot. Gerald pushed his way right up to the porch where a policeman was standing. "Who got shot?" Gerald demanded.

"Well, we think the boy's name was Floyd Gore and we think his friend, Eddie Kraus, was the one who accidentally shot him," the policeman said.

"Is Floyd going to be all right?" Gerald asked. "It all depends on how fast they get him to the hospital," the policeman answered. "He was hit right in the face."

I couldn't believe it. Both Floyd and Eddie had worked with me as ushers at the Bailey. As a matter of fact, they were still working there. After the police left, I wandered back home still hoping Floyd would be okay.

An article in the Star News the next day revealed all the details of the shooting. Eddie, Floyd, Jimmy Dosher, Danny Davis, and Edward Strayhorn had been upstairs playing cards. Five other boys were downstairs, also playing cards, when they heard the shot. Eddie had gotten a .22 caliber pistol, owned by his father, from a cabinet and was playing with the gun.

According to the boys who witnessed the accident, Floyd asked Eddie not to point the gun at him. Eddie replied the safety was on and the gun wasn't loaded. A second later, the gun went off with the bullet hitting Floyd in the chin. He was dead on arrival at the hospital.

As a result of the shooting, Eddie suffered from a nervous breakdown. The other boys who had been present suffered from nightmares for a long time. Everyone in Dry Pond knew both Floyd and Eddie and the tragedy was taken very hard by the community.

Chapter 26
The Cold War Goes On

The shooting was still on everyone's minds when some good news was received. After three years of fighting, the Korean War ended. It began on June 25, 1950 and an armistice was concluded on July 27, 1953. Although the war didn't affect a lot of Wilmingtonians, everyone knew somebody who knew somebody who had been wounded or killed. The newspapers' leading articles for three years were about the war.

General Douglas MacArthur, hero of World War II, was replaced as commander of the Allied forces in April, 1951, when he wanted to extend the war into China by bombing missions there. President Harry Truman didn't agree with General MacArthur's plans and finally fired him and replaced him with General Matthew Ridgeway. President Truman was afraid MacArthur's plans would bring China to throw its military might into the war although China was already supplying North Korea with advice and support as well as some covert troops.

The firing of General MacArthur caused quite a stir. When he returned to the States, parades were held in his honor and he was asked to speak before Congress. His speech contained a sentence that became famous "Old soldiers never die, they just fade away."

As young men in 1953 were faced with the prospect of being drafted and perhaps being sent to Korea, the NHHS senior boys were doubly glad the war had ended. It wouldn't be too bad to be drafted as long as the US wasn't involved in an active war.

The Cold War was at its coldest in the summer of 1953 even though the Korean War was over. NHHS students didn't overly concern themselves with the Cold War other than reading daily reports in the newspaper or listening to radio news broadcasts.

The federal government even made a film, *Duck and Cover,* that was designed to show children how to react in the event of an atomic attack by Russia. However, the cartoon turtle, the cheerful theme song, and the practical advice that was supposed to reassure children mostly succeeded in frightening them even more. The images of little Johnny diving off his bicycle convinced them the bombs could fall at any moment and gave them nightmares.

The US Air Force kept huge B-52 bombers, loaded with atomic and hydrogen bombs, in the air twenty-four hours a day near the Soviet border so that an immediate response could be made if the Russians attacked us.

As a result of the constant reminder, in the papers and on the radio, of how close we were to nuclear annihilation, NHHS students, like everyone else, had some feeling of dread in their subconscious mind.

On June 19, 1953, we were faced with the reality of the Cold War when two American spies, Julius and Ethel Rosenberg were executed for passing secret documents about the atomic bomb to the Russian NKVD. No American spy had been executed since 1945 and the Rosenbergs were the first and last civilian spies executed for treason.

Even if we were subconsciously worrying about nuclear annihilation, we had to go on with our lives, which we were able to do.

Chapter 27
Life of a Soda Jerk

In July, 1953, I was able to get a job as a soda jerk at Futrelle's Pharmacy on the northwest corner of Second and Princess Streets. A friend of mine, Jimmy Forrester, who worked at Futrelle's helped me land this plush job. The hours were much better than those at the Baily. I didn't have to work at night or on Sundays.

In addition to having a pharmacy, Futrelle's also had a soda fountain where all types of drinks were served as well as sandwiches and other snacks. Futrelle's was heavily patronized by all the people who worked in the surrounding area. At lunch time, it was a beehive of activity. Many attorneys and other court officials came to Futrelle's every day for a quick lunch. There were three or four tables with chairs inside the store.

We served four basic sandwiches; chicken salad for $.15, ham salad, egg salad, and pimento cheese for $.10. It didn't cost an arm and a leg to eat there. The salads were made in the mornings in a room on the second floor. I don't believe the Health Department ever inspected that room. If it had, Futrelle's may have gone out of the sandwich business

The soda jerks put the various ingredients of each salad into a dishpan and stirred them with their hands until the salad was mixed thoroughly. Mr. Futrelle encouraged us to use rubber gloves but that was such a nuisance, we generally didn't use them.

Jimmy asked me one day "Have you ever noticed the size of Mr. Futrelle's feet? People tell me he has the biggest feet in Wilmington." I hadn't given much thought to Mr. Futrelle's feet until then but after that I couldn't seem to keep my eyes off his feet. They really were huge.

Mr. Leon Futrelle was easy to work for. He would give me time off whenever I needed to participate with the NHHS swim team. He gave me a great complement one day as I was upstairs mixing the chicken salad ingredients.

"You know, Kenan, you really do a good job making that chicken salad. You don't mind getting your hands dirty."

Many businessmen and county employees ate lunch at Futrelle's Pharmacy. The courthouse was only one block away. Futrelle's wasn't a fast-food restaurant but the soda-jerks could make a chicken-salad sandwich and a milkshake in no time at all. Futrelle's was one of former mayor J. E. L. "Hi Buddy" Wade's favorite spots. Mayor E. S. Capps, as well as attorney Aaron Goldberg and Recorder's Court Solicitor Johnny Walker, also ate lunch there several times a week.

Many downtown restaurants and cafeterias offered delicious food to shoppers and workers: Dixie Restaurant at 115 Princess St; H & W Cafeteria at 118 Princess St; Puritan Restaurant at 133 Market St; None-Such Restaurant at 123 Market St; Friendly Cafeteria at 111 Chestnut St; Saffo's Restaurant at 249 N. Front St; and the Jiffy Grill at 206 N. Front St., to mention just a few.

With each job I had, I evaluated it to determine if there was a future in it for me. I knew I didn't want to be a soda jerk all my life so I had some conversations with the pharmacist. The mixing of all the powders and liquids into medications people depended on for their health seemed like a worthwhile vocation. I was disappointed to learn a pharmacist had to have a college degree. I asked the pharmacist one day "How hard can it be to count out pills and put them in a bottle?" He seemed offended. I knew I could never afford to go to college so I crossed pharmacist off my list.

I didn't like wearing the little cap and the white shirt with a bow tie. It seemed each job I got I had to wear some silly looking outfit. However, soda jerking wasn't bad and I worked at Futrelle's until I graduated from NHHS in May, 1954.

As I didn't have to work on Sundays that gave me time to head for Wrightsville Beach on some Sunday afternoons usually with my two friends, Vernon and Leonard. As neither of us had a car, we rode the city bus. We always went to the Lumina Pavilion. There were locker rooms in which you could change clothing. There was also a ten pin bowling alley, among other games, on the ground floor.

We loved to bowl but scoring very high with ten pins was beyond our bowling ability. The pin boys were never very helpful. If they had wanted to, they could have accidentally tipped over the seven and ten pins with hardly any effort. Many times, they failed to place the pins in the right spot. I thought how hard can that can be. I believed I could have been a super pin boy if I set my mind to it.

I loved to body surf. Surfers with real surf boards were a rarity. I don't recall ever seeing any surf boards although I read somewhere the first surfing contest was held in Wrightsville Beach in the 1920's. [11]

An event occurred in June, 1953, that had a major impact on the lives of everyone in New Hanover and surrounding counties. Dan Cameron, who was Mayor Pro Tem of Wilmington, announced the two radio stations in Wilmington, WMFD and WGNI, had joined together to file an application with the Federal Communications Commission to establish a television station in Wilmington.

Richard Dunlea, the manager of WMFD, and Sam Brody, the president of WGNI, both expressed hopes that by joining together in the application, it would be granted quickly. It was and WMFD-TV first began telecasting on April 9, 1954.

WGNI was the favorite radio station of NHHS students. It featured several programs from the Mutual Broadcasting System but it was Paul Parker and Lou Essick that attracted young people. The two disc jockeys played all the top hits of the day; Paul Parker in the morning and Lou Essick in the afternoons.

On Friday, July 10, 1953, Alton Lennon was appointed by Governor William Umstead to fill the remaining term of Senator Willis Smith who died in June, 1953. Senator Lennon was the father of one of my classmates, Edna Lee Lennon. I wasn't a close friend of hers but it was exciting to know I was a classmate of the daughter of an US Senator.

The American Legion baseball team had a good season in the summer of 1953. They won the Eastern Division of the state of North Carolina by defeating the team from Siler City. However, in the state finals, the team lost to Cherryville in seven games. The Eastern championship was the first for Wilmington since Legion baseball began in Wilmington.

---

[11] When I was a member of the Wrightsville Beach Jaycees in 1965, we sponsored a surfing contest, the first one in modern times. The contest concluded with a social in the ball room at the Lumina.

Some of the players were: Mac McPherson, Derris Bradshaw, Scotty Hurst, Bubba Pursley, Neil Easom, Jimmy Shaw, Harry Odham, Clifton Patton, Bobby Edison, Tommy Shannon, and Hookie Hales.

Chapter 28
Mule Riding

Before school began in the fall of 1953, Vernon wanted to take Leonard and me to visit some of his relatives who lived a few miles south of Wallace along Highway 117. Vernon had recently gotten his driver's license and sometimes was allowed by his Daddy to use his truck that was used to pick up scrap metal for sale to Queensboro Steel Co.

The cab could be disconnected from the trailer when not being used in the scrap metal business so it was about the same as driving a pick-up truck. However, it was a great big cab with a front bench seat wide enough to seat four people if they didn't mind sitting scrunched up.

We enjoyed the ride from Wilmington to the cousin's house. On our way, we stopped at Paul's Place near Rocky Point to get some of their wonderful hot dogs along with a Pepsi-Cola. Vernon was a good driver but occasionally when changing gears, we could hear the gears scraping. The truck had several forward gears and it was quite a challenge to finally get the truck in its final forward gear.

We arrived at the cousin's house in the middle of the afternoon and he and his family were very surprised, but happy, to see us. We sat on their front porch and carried on very interesting, stimulating conversations for some time.

As we were about ready to leave, Vernon asked his cousin. "Does your neighbor still have his old mule, Jack? I used to like to ride him around the farm when we lived here."

His cousin answered, "Oh, yeah. Jack is still going strong. I don't know what Percy would do without him. Say, if you'd like to ride him again, why don't you ride across the road to see Percy? He'll probably be happy to let you and your friends take a ride on Jack. I would go with you but I promised my wife I'd take her to Wallace this afternoon to the B & S

Sandwich Shop for a hamburger. Why don't you and your friends go on over there and take a ride?"

That sounded like a good plan to Vernon so we climbed up into the truck cab and rode across the road to the Percy's house. We were disappointed to find him not home but Vernon felt confident he wouldn't mind if we took Jack out for a short ride.

Vernon got the bridle which was hanging on a nail and slipped it over Jack's head and led him outside. Somehow, just as he got outside, Jack threw his head around, the bridle came off, and Jack ran off through some nearby woods.

Vernon began running after the mule with Leonard and me following. We got up close to Jack in two or three minutes but Jack wouldn't let Vernon get close enough to put on the bridle. He would edge away a few feet or run again through the woods out of sight.

We chased Jack for almost two hours through the woods, across fields, across ditches until we finally trapped him in the corner of a neighbor's fenced in pasture. We were all exhausted, including Jack. It took us thirty minutes to walk back to Percy's barn where Jack was led in and the door slammed shut.

Our mule-riding excursion turned out to be something less than pleasurable. We were scratched, muddy, with beggar lice all over our clothing. I made a resolution to never again go with Vernon to see his cousin. On our way back home, we stopped again at Paul's Place and his hot dogs restored our energy and spirits. We agreed Paul's Place hot dogs were much tastier than the cold, soggy hot dogs at Pete's Place, a favorite lunch spot for some NHHS students.

Just as we were about to leave Paul's Place, a Pender County Sheriff's car came roaring by with its siren blasting. The car pulled into the parking lot of a combination café and service station just across Highway 133. The deputy sheriff jumped out his car and ran inside.

We were very curious as to what was going on so the three of us ran across Highway 133 to the store. After getting inside we learned that someone had robbed the store a few minutes earlier at gun point. The robber had come into the store, put some coins into the juke box, and selected the hit song "*From*

Rags to Riches" by Tony Bennett. While it was playing, he pulled out a pistol and made the owner empty the cash register. He then fled in a 1949 Studebaker in the direction of Long Creek.

The owner was naturally upset but he had to admit the robber had a sense of humor.

Chapter 29
Our Sixth Move

Just as I was getting settled in at 407 Church Street, Mother decided it was time for us to move again. I wasn't sure why she thought we should move but move we did, this time to an apartment at 10 ½ South Seventh Street, between Market and Dock Streets. I liked the move because now I only had to walk five and one-half blocks to school. I could sleep a little later in the mornings and had a little more time at home in the afternoons.

It was an old but nice house. Mrs. Carolyn Henly, a real estate agent, lived in the right-side apartment while we lived in the left-side. At this time there were six in my family living there. I believe Mrs. Henly's peace and tranquility may have been disturbed at times by Gerald and Coleman's rowdy friends that visited them quite often.

One afternoon as Gerald and I were sitting on the front steps, discussing world affairs, we saw Coleman and a close friend of his, Joey Starling, come running from the direction of Market Street. Gerald yelled at them as they ran by "What's going on? Is something after you?" They didn't stop to answer but ran up the driveway to the rear of the house.

Just as they disappeared, a car came up from the direction of Market Street and stopped in front of us. I saw the passenger in the car was a classmate of mine, Joyce Whitman. She and her family lived just up the street on the north side of Market. A man, whom I assumed to be her father, asked. "Did y'all see two little boys run by? They were out on Market Street throwing grapes at cars. Just look at the mess on my windshield!"

Gerald and I looked at each other and Gerald answered. "Yes, sir, we did and I think they ran on down the street out of sight." Gerald could think fast in times of emergency.

"Well," Mr. Whitman said. "If you see them again, tell them they'd better quit throwing grapes or the police are going to be after them." We nodded our heads in acquiescence.

They left and Gerald and I went back into our house. It wasn't but a few minutes later when I looked out my upstairs bedroom window and saw Coleman and Joey come out of the driveway and walk rapidly towards Market Street. I could see their pockets were bulging with grapes. They had replenished their supply of ammunition from a grapevine in the back yard.

Before I could run downstairs and out onto the porch, they were already out of sight. About twenty minutes later, they came running back and disappeared behind our house. Our neighbor, Mrs. Henly, drove up and asked me where Coleman and his friend were. She repeated the same story as that of Mr. Whitman. Coleman and Joey were out on Market Street throwing grapes at cars.

Unfortunately for Coleman and Joey, Mrs. Henly recognized Coleman and followed him home. I didn't see any way out for Coleman, so I went to the back yard and found him and Joey hiding behind a storage shed. I told them Mrs. Henly had recognized Coleman and they may as well as come out and face the music.

Coleman asked pitifully "What's she gonna do to us? Grapes cain't do hardly any damage to a car, can they?"

"I don't know what she might do but you've got to come talk to her," I said.

They did come out after they had carefully emptied their pockets of their reserve ammunition. As it turned out, Mrs. Henly wasn't as severe on them as she might have been. She said a few words that put the fear of God in them and got them to promise to stop engaging in grape warfare on Market Street They stuck to their promise but found other ways to get into trouble, or to cause trouble for others.

Jimmy Pappas, a classmate, told me that his father, the minister of St. Nicholas Greek Orthodox Church which was just across Orange Street from the Community Center, was thinking about cutting down their pomegranate tree. It seems that the tree wasn't producing fruit that summer although it always had been very fruitful. Father Pappas told Jimmy he was going to follow what Jesus said as found in the book of Matthew, Chapter 7, Verse 19, King James Version: *"Every tree that does not bear good fruit is cut down and thrown into the fire."* Jimmy said he had persuaded his father to give the tree one more year.

Little did they know that Coleman and Joey had discovered the pomegranates were delicious and had been sneaking into Father Pappas' back yard and snitching the fruit.

Chapter 30
The Macao Light

I turned age 17 on August 31, 1953, and was ready to begin my senior year at NHHS. I was getting older but wasn't sure I was any wiser. Joan suggested to me I should look up what my astrological sign portended for me.

In my first week back during a study hall in the school library, I asked Miss Fannie O'Keefe, the librarian, if she could help me find a book that discussed astrological signs. She apparently knew where every book in the library was. Without any hesitation, she led me to the book shelf where she pulled out a book entitled *Astrology and You.*

I quickly found the section that dealt with my Zodiac sign, Virgo. I read Virgo people were loyal, kind, hardworking, and practical but were also shy, tended to worry, and were overly critical of self and others. They disliked rudeness, asking for help or taking center stage. They were conservative and liked to be organized. While Virgos could be worrywarts, they did their best to temper these impulses. There was nothing in there about dancing.

That didn't sound too bad but it offered me no clue as to what I may be when and if I ever grew up. I liked the part that said Virgo people were conservative and liked to be organized. With my limited knowledge of bookkeeping and accounting, that field seemed to be appealing to me. So in my senior year, two of the courses I signed up for were typing and bookkeeping. Miss Julia Bray was my typing teacher and Mrs. Mary Hood taught bookkeeping.

Some of my other classes were chemistry under Mr. Haywood Bellamy, Government under Mr. C. D. Gurganous, French II under Mr. T. G. (Tiny Gorilla) Browning, and English Grammar under Mrs. Doris Hovis.

Several of my friends took an art class under Miss Emma Lossen. After viewing the artwork of some of them, I assumed they had skipped the majority of classes. Miss Lossen was a great art teacher as well as being a great humanitarian.

There was a student at NHHS who was originally from the Ukraine, Tamara Osikowska. She had been forced to leave her home in the Ukraine at the age of eight with her family and had spent some years in concentration camps in Germany. After the war, she had applied for entrance to the United States through the Displaced Persons program. Miss Lossen somehow learned of Tamara and had adopted her as her daughter. Not many NHHS students had a story to tell that would compare with Tamara's. It was even worse than growing up in Chinquapin.

It seemed each teacher of the subjects I took loved to make homework assignments. That necessitated carrying four or five heavy books back and forth from home to school each day. Backpacks were an unheard of book carrying aid. We either carried two or three in each hand or hugged them to our chest, a girly thing to do.

One of the first things all incoming seniors did was to walk up the Senior Steps. The first day of school the steps were very busy with the new seniors walking up and down even though a shorter route would have been to use the stairs at either end of the school building. We had waited three long years to exercise that privilege.

Each student had a locker but it was usually in a rather inconvenient place. My classrooms were deliberately chosen based on the distance they were from my locker.

I heard a lot of my school friends talk about the fun they had by looking for the Maco Light. The story was that back in the 1800's, an Atlantic Coastline Railroad brakeman, Joe Baldwin, had accidentally been run over by the train and his head had been severed. Years after the accident, people began seeing what was reputed to be the ghost of Joe Baldwin walking along the rails, swinging his lantern, looking for his head. The Maco Light had been investigated thoroughly not only by local news reporters but had also been written about by some national publications.

One Saturday evening when my friends and I didn't have anything else to do, we decided to take a ride across the river to Maco and look for the Maco Light.

On our trip, there was Vernon, Leonard, Joe Tardugno, and myself. Vernon was able to get his Daddy's old truck cab and the four of us squeezed in. It didn't take long to get to Maco and then turn into the woods where the best viewing spot was located. We got out and saw there were several other vehicles that had brought ghost hunters to the site.

We didn't see anything at first until the four of us began walking down the tracks towards Wilmington. Suddenly a group of kids came running back up the tracks. They looked as if they had seen a ghost. I thought I recognized some of them as then ran past but they were running so fast and it was dark so I wasn't sure.

I read the next day in the Teen Age Tattler that a Sunday school class of Lake Forest Baptist church had a wiener roast followed by a hayride to see the Maco light.

Patsy Barrett wrote that Ann Meadows and Harold Manning, Clara Loftin and Johnny Hinnant, Hilda Young and Gary Preston, Tommy Capps and Jo Ann Lennon, Shirley Rollinson and Jerry Coleman, Peggy Blackburn and Jimmy Rice, Jackie Huffman and Danny Parham, Eleanor Walton and Dickie Benton, Frances Paretti and Pat Benson, Nancy Brown and Jerry Ely, Earl Brown and Ada Eubanks had an exciting trip to see the Maco light.

As we continued walking, suddenly we saw what appeared to be a bright light ahead of us but some distance away. We walked and then ran towards the light but we could never get any closer. It just kept retreating down the tracks. If we walked back towards the parking site, the light seemed to follow us.

After playing this game for about an hour with the light, we decided we had seen enough of the Maco Light and rode back to Wilmington. When I told other friends what we had seen, some of them were skeptical but others said they had also seen the Maco Light. Some of the Lake Forest Baptist Church group backed up my story.

Chapter 33
My Senior Year Begins

The NHHS football team got off to a good start in the 1953 season by defeating the Asheville Lee Edwards High School team, 16 – 13, in their opening game on September 5, 1953. Stars for the Wildcats were quarterback Jimmy Williams, running backs Rex Hardy, Tommy Shannon, and Tommy Millard. Derris Bradshaw kicked the extra points and linemen Wayne Cushing, Ken Grant, Jimmy Edwards, Tex Jordan and Boyce Cole were outstanding.

Derris Bradshaw and H. F. McPherson were the smallest players on the team while Jim Durant at 215 pounds, Bob Coleman at 205, George McEachern and Roger Seitter at 200 were the largest.

While I was an usher at the Bailey Theatre, I had seen hundreds of movies, many of them dozens of times. When I learned Charles Laughton would appear in the NHHS auditorium on the evening of Saturday, November 28, 1953, I decided I had to see his performance. His role as Captain Bligh in the movie *Mutiny on the Bounty* had impressed me. He also had starred in another hit movie, *The Hunchback of Notre Dame*, which I hadn't enjoyed so much. In that movie, he played the part of Quasimodo, the hunchback. Quasimodo's love for Esmeralda, played by Maureen O'Hara, required a stretch of the imagination.

His show, *An Evening with Charles Laughton,* showed him in an entirely different light. He read, or pretended to read, parts of books which he had memorized including the *Book of Job, Song of Solomon,* and whole chapters of writings by Thomas Wolfe, Mark Twain, Charles Dickens and James Thurber.

I tried to get Vernon, Leonard, and even Gerald to go with me but they weren't interested in Charles Laughton. I went by myself and had the misfortune to sit in front of two English teachers, Miss Frances Formyduval and Mrs. Doris Hovis. After the performance when they asked how I enjoyed it, I had to tell a little fib so they wouldn't think I didn't appreciate high culture. As I walked home, I thought how wise Vernon, Leonard and Gerald had been.

Things were beginning to get organized at NHHS in September. The different clubs and organizations were appointing or electing their officers and leaders. I was even elected President of Mr. T. G. Browning's French Class. We cleverly named the club *Le Bonne Heure* which means happy hour. Happy Hour in Mrs. Browning's class wasn't what most people think of when they hear about a Happy Hour. It wasn't always a happy hour in there under the thumb of Tiny Gorilla.

Ethel Avera was elected Vice-President and Carolyn Cotchett was elected Secretary-Treasurer. I wasn't sure why we needed a treasurer as I don't recall the class ever having any funds.

Many students followed the Wildcats for out-of-town games. As games were on Friday nights, getting back home in the early AM on Saturday morning wasn't harmful to school work. Attendance at the Goldsboro game in October, 1953, was unusually large due to the Atlantic Coast Line Service Club sponsoring a train from Wilmington to Goldsboro solely to provide transportation to the game.

The train left Wilmington at 5:30 PM and arrived in Goldsboro at 7:30 PM. After the game, the train departed Goldsboro at 11 PM and got back to Wilmington at 1 AM. The cost of the round-trip ticket was very low so that practically all students could afford to go. It was a noisy, raucous train ride there and back; especially back because the Wildcats won the game 13-7.

On November 17th, during the chapel program, the Hanoverian staff conducted the selection of superlatives for the Class of 1954. With the theme from the TV show "*Dragnet*," playing in the background, George Autry, Margaret Head, Carolyn Cole, Loretta Berlin, Anita Culver, Patty Register, Elizabeth Barefoot and Karen Kurka went out into the audience and found the winners and escorted them back to the stage.

Best Looking were Bobby Johnston and Margaret Rowe; Friendliest were Larry Bullard and Betty Bordeaux; Best Personality were Barbara Pace and Bob Godley; Most

Original were Hal Johnson and Jo Debnam; Most Likely to Succeed were Jimmy Williams and Ann Pate; Most Intellectual were Sherri Forrester and Joe Tardugno; Wittiest were Douglas Upchurch and Sally Hicks; Most School Spirit were Don Frost and Roxana Mebane; Most Athletic were Derris Bradshaw and Jo Ann Jordan; Best Dressed were Bubba Pursley and Margaret Thompson; Best All Around were Pete Land and Pat Tickner; and Most Dependable were David Barefoot and Patsy Barrett.

As I sat in my seat and saw the superlative winners stand on the stage, I envied them. They were all outstanding students and highly respected by their classmates and teachers. I tried to imagine myself being selected as the most outstanding in some category that was not on the agenda.

I thought if they had a category as the Most Shy Student, or the Worst Dancer, I would have been chosen. If they had a category for the student who Made The Most Chicken Salad Sandwiches, I would have been chosen. And if they had a category for the student who had Cropped The Most Tobacco, I would have won that superlative, hands down.

I thought of several other superlatives that I could have won but other than those four, I realized the others I thought of were silly.

I had really wanted to do well academically my final year at NHHS so when the first report period for the 1953/1954 year ended, I was sure I would be on the first honor roll. I was disappointed when I learned I only made the second honor roll.

When I saw who had made the first honor roll, a few names on the list surprised me. Betty Ann Bordeaux, Clifford Comeau, Ann Croom, Jimmy Forrester, Sherri Forrester, Lloyd Harrison, Ginger Keister, Hattie Kinlaw, Karen Kurka, Mary Mintz, Bob Murphey, Jimmy Pappas, Charlene Ray, Pat Register, Sue Walton, Al Wiley, and Jimmy Williams must have applied themselves diligently when it didn't appear to me some of them were trying that hard.

Although I didn't make the first honor roll for the first report period, I made it for the second. In addition to the students who made the honor roll for the first period, fifteen other seniors who didn't do so well in that period buckled down and made it in the second report period: Jennie Lee Batlettt, Nancy Bates, Norma Bryant, Sybil Canady, Carolyn Cole, Emily Gilbert, Rita Hodges, Dottie Jo James, Barbara McKee, Mary Neal, Sally Ottaway, Joe Tardugno, Lim Vallianos, Bobby Warwick, and last but least, Kenan Maready.

On December 8, 1953, a goal I had set for myself a year earlier was realized; I was inducted into the National Honor Society right there on the stage in the school auditorium in front of the entire student body. I was rather proud or myself.

Others inducted that day were: Ethel Avera, Jennie Lee Bartlett, Loretta Berlin, Carolyn Cole, Carolyn Cotchett, Anita Culver, Jimmy Forrester, Betty Garvis, Emily Gilbert, Marie Hall, Peggy Hewett, Rita Hodges, Dottie Jo James, Hattie Kinlaw, Mary Mintz, Barbara Pace, Patricia Register, Lynn Shannon, Gloria Smith, Betty Thompson, and Tamara Osikowska.

Chapter 34
A Swimming Scholarship?

The swimming team for NHHS, the Aquacats, didn't have as much support as did the football team. The swimmers practiced just as hard and tried just as hard but swimming didn't create the excitement as did football and basketball.

Grier White had tried to get me to try out for the swim team for the school year 1952-1953 but I couldn't find the time at that point in my life. I enjoyed swimming. I had learned to swim at a very early age in Halso Swamp, Cypress Creek at Cleveland's Bridge, at Deep Bottom, at White Lake and in the Northeast Cape Fear River at Chinquapin. I had even saved three boys from drowning in the river.

One of our more impressive meets, although we lost, was one with the swim team at East Carolina College. The team from ECC won the last event to come out ahead, 36-30. But as we were competing against a college team, we felt pretty good.

Billy Wall finished second in the 50 yard free style event; Oscar Grant finished second in the 100 yard breast stroke event; Tommy Penney finished third in the 200 yard free style event; Mike Mallory won the 100 yard back stroke event; I finished second in the 100 yard free style event; Grier White won the 150 yard individual medley event; and the 200 yard relay event was won by the NHHS team with me, Albert Creasy, Billy Wall, and Jimmy Hickman.

We had a fairly successful year, winning some meets but unfortunately also losing some. Swimming was an exhausting sport. The combination of exhaustion and the smell and taste of chlorine in the water almost always made me sick to my stomach. I felt the urge to throw up as I finished the final lap in an event.

My usual routine was to pull myself out of the pool, run to the locker room and throw up. I noticed a few of my teammates also had the same problem. The locker room had a very bad odor during the swim meets, even worse than usual.

Although I threw up a lot, apparently the swim coach at East Carolina was impressed with my ability as I received, in late February, an invitation from him to visit the college for the purpose of discussing the possibility of being given a swimming scholarship. Grier White also received a similar letter so we made plans to visit with the coach on Friday, February 26. I didn't have access to a car, of course, but Grier was allowed to use the family car.

We arrived at East Carolina around 11 a.m. and the coach took us on a tour of the campus. We ate lunch with him in the college cafeteria, talked some more and left for home about 2:30 p.m. He told us he would send us a letter in a few days with his decision as to whether or not to offer us a scholarship.

On the way back to Wilmington, I asked Grier to take a route that would put us in Chinquapin about 4 p.m. I wanted to have one more hot dog in Billy Brinkley's store. He agreed to do that. When we walked into the store, Billy and Margaret were behind the café counter, just as I remembered them from three years earlier. The old TV set was still on in the dry goods section of the store. It still didn't have a good picture, mostly snow and an image that flitted across the screen occasionally.

Billy and Margaret were glad to see me and we talked about old times as Grier and I ate our hot dogs. Grier had to admit Billy's hot dogs were better than Paul's Place and much better than Pete's Place hot dogs.

As we were finishing up, a carload of boys drove up and came in. I recognized them right away as they were old childhood friends; Jimmy Halso, Toogie Futreal, Raymond Earl Cottle and Elwood Lanier. They had dropped in to shoot a few games of pool in Billy's pool room.

I had lived with Jimmy and his family for a few weeks in January, 1951, while I finished the first semester of that school year at Chinquapin School. He had been my best friend when we lived in the Mill Swamp and Chinquapin area.

I had also lived with Toogie and his family during the summer of 1952. At that time, my only skill that allowed me to earn money was cropping tobacco. Toogie's father was kind enough to hire me to do that very thing that summer.

All the boys that came into Billy's played on the Chinquapin basketball team, a team I would have been on had my family not moved to Wilmington. Just by chance, the Duplin County basketball tournament had recently finished a couple of days earlier. I had read in the paper Chinquapin had beaten the Wallace Bulldogs, the most feared team in the Duplin County Conference.

"Hey, Jimmy," I said. "I'm glad to see you and Toogie and Raymond Earl. I read in the paper the other day Chinquapin beat the Wallace Bulldogs in the county tournament and that you outscored Wray Carlton, 18 – 14. Is it true that he's got a football scholarship to play for Duke?"

Jimmy gave me a hug, right there in front of the other boys. "That's what we've heard. But he's better in football than in basketball. Did you read that we lost the next night to Calypso? I guess we were too confident after beating the top-seeded team."

That gave me an idea. "Think about this," I said. "I play on a team in the City League in Wilmington. We're not as good as a high school team but we're not too bad. We call our team the Wolverines. Do you think we could come up here one evening and play the Chinquapin team, just for fun?"

"Oh, yeah," he replied. "Don't you think so?" He asked the other boys. They were all in favor of the idea. Before Grier and I left for Wilmington, we set a date, Friday, March 6 for the game. Jimmy said he would let the student body know about the game and was sure there would be a large crowd on hand.

When Grier dropped me off at my home, Mother was anxious to hear about my meeting with the swimming coach. She desperately wanted her children to go to college but our financial condition wouldn't allow that to happen.   She was hoping the coach would give me a full scholarship. I told her the coach would write me in a few days.

We waited anxiously for the letter to arrive. When I got home after school on Thursday, Mother was waiting at the front door with a letter from East Carolina College. I tore the letter open. The offer was for a partial scholarship, for tuition only. The cost of books, meals, and a room would have to be paid by me.   It couldn't be done.   We were greatly disappointed but agreed that if I really applied myself and made good grades the rest of the year, surely I could get a good job after graduating. There had to be a lot of businesses in Wilmington that needed someone who had cropped tobacco, ushered at a first class theatre, and worked as a soda jerk at Futrelle's Pharmacy.

When the next Friday arrived, the day of our basketball game with Chinquapin, Leonard and I rode to Chinquapin with Vernon in his father's old junk truck. I thought it was a little undignified to return to Chinquapin is such a vehicle but I didn't have any other way of getting there.

The other three boys rode with Bob Coleman in his father's car; Joe Tardugno, Jimmy Pappas and Marvin Watson.

We arrived at the school and parked in front of the old gymnasium.   My grandfather, John Bryant Maready, had donated the lumber that was used to build the building back in the 1920's.

Chinquapin School

The crowd wasn't as large as we had expected. Jimmy came over to me and began apologizing. As it turned out, the school authorities wouldn't permit the school team to play a game against a non-sanctioned team. I never was able to fully understand the reason. Jimmy was able to get a team together but it consisted of boys who played basketball but were not on the school team: Lenwood Simpson, James Hunter, J. T. Cavenaugh, Jaycee Williams, and a few others that I didn't know.

Needless to say, we won the game easily. In the sparse crowd, there were a few girls I wanted to show off for: Christine Sholar, Grace Dail, Rita Rae Jones, Faye Walton, Shirley Brown, Yvonne Sandlin. etc. Unfortunately, I didn't have one of my better games. I couldn't seem to make a basket, even an uncontested layup.

Our team didn't run plays, we just played free-lance. What each of us had on our minds was to be the high scorer and get our names in the Star-News. We really hated to give the ball up because we may never get it back.

My dream of showing off before my old friends in Chinquapin didn't come true.

Chapter 33
The Aquacats

Just before our Christmas holidays began, the Aquacats had their final match of 1953; an exhibition meet against the Alumni Aquacats. In the 50 yard freestyle, alumnus Pete Dannenbaum finished first while setting a new pool record. I finished second in that event.

In the 100 yard breast stroke event, alumnus Fritz Oertel finished first while Oscar Grant finished second and Jimmy Hickmon finished third.

In the 200 yard freestyle event, alumnus Eric Oertel finished first and Jimmy Hickmon finished second. In the 100 yard backstroke event, alumnus Smitty Jewell finished first while setting a new pool record while Freddy Smith finished second.

In the 100 yard freestyle event, alumnus Sam McMillan finished first while setting a new point record. I finished second and Albert Creasey finished third.

In the 150 yard medley relay, the NHHS team with Freddy Smith, Oscar Grant, and Jimmy Hickmon won while the Alumni team finished second.

In the final event, the 200 yard freestyle relay, the Alumni team won while setting a new pool record with the NHHS team consisting of Albert Creasey, Oscar Grant, Jimmy Hickmon and myself finishing second.

The final score of the match was the Alumni Aquacats with 28 points while the current Aquacats finished with 25 points.

The Aquacats continued their season in a meet with the swim team from Fayetteville High School. We won the match easily, 49-17. As usual there were very few spectators. Swimming just wasn't as exciting as football or basketball.

Billy Wall and Albert Creasy finished first and second in the 50 yard freestyle event. Oscar Grant and the swimmer from Fayetteville finished in a dead heat in the 100 yard breast stroke event. In the 200 yard freestyle event, the Fayetteville swimmer won with Tommy Penny coming in second and Jimmy Hickman finishing third. Freddy Smith won the 100 yard backstroke event. I won the 100 yard freestyle event with Ed Veazey finishing second. Grier White won the 150 yard individual medley event and Jan Williams won the diving competition. The 200 yard freestyle team, with Jimmy Hickmon, Albert Creasy, Billy Wall and I, beat out Fayetteville.

As I was entered in only two events in that match, I only threw up two times.

On the final day when the holidays began, all NHHS students headed home for a much needed few days rest and relaxation.

1953 Top Songs, Movies and Books

Top Ten Songs
 Song from Moulin Rouge by Percy Faith
 Vaya Con Dios by Less Paul and Mary Ford
 Doggie in the Window by Patti Page
 I'm Walking Behind You by EddieFisher
 You, You, You by the Ames Brothers
 Till I Waltz Again With You by Teresa Brewer
 April In Portugal by Les Baxter
 No Other Love by Perry Como
 Don't Let the Stars Get in Your Eyes by Perry Como
 I Believe by Frankie Laine

Top Five Movies
 The Robe with Richard Burton and Jean Simmons
 From Here To Eternity with Burt Lancaster , Deborah Kerr
     Montgomery Clift, Frank Sinatra and Donna Reed
 Shane with Alan Ladd, Van Heflin and Brandon deWilde
 How To Marry A Millionaire with Marilyn Monore,
     Betty Grable, Lauren Bacall and William Powell
 Peter Pan with Bobby Driscoll, Kathryn Beaumont,
     Hans Conried, Paul Colins, and Heather Angel

Top Five Books
 The Robe by Lloyd C. Douglas
 Desiree by Annemarie Selinko
 Battle Cry by Leon Uris
 From Here to Eternity by James Jones
 The High and the Mighty by Ernest K. Gann

Chapter 34
Spring of 1954

The holidays passed much too quickly for me. I didn't seem to get as much rest and relaxation as I had wanted. The truth was I didn't feel ready to take the mid-term exams. During the few days out of school, I had forgotten almost everything I had learned, I didn't relish the thought of cramming so much knowledge into my already overburdened brain.

Regardless of the state of my relaxation, school began. During the holidays, a lot of progress had been made on the new addition to New Hanover High School, now known as Brogden Hall, on the corner of Market and Thirteenth Streets. It seemed construction had been going on forever. The basketball arena part was supposed to have been ready for the basketball season in the fall of 1953 but numerous delays had resulted in the contractor getting far behind schedule.

Unfortunately, for students who loved the hot dogs, etc., at Pete's Place, this famous eating establishment had to be torn down to make room for the new building. Realizing that Pete's would no longer be there to meet the nutritional needs of NHHS and Wilmington College students, Mr. Herbert Fisher built at the corner of Twelfth and Princess Streets another grill and soda shop which he named the Varsity Grill. It proved to be a tremendous success.

Our class of 1954 was the last class that didn't get to use the new building. The basketball arena would have the largest seating capacity of any east of Reynolds Coliseum in Raleigh. It would seat 4,376 for basketball, 5,115 for stage presentations and 5,700 for convention events.

The people most responsible for getting it built were Coach Leon Brogden, Superintendent of Schools, H. M. Roland, Board of Education Chairman, Dr. John T. Hoggard, NHHS Principal, Dale Spencer, and Mr. J. C. Roe of the High School Athletic Board.

Early in January, 1954, the news story that attracted a lot of attention in southeastern North Carolina was the story about the "Bladenboro Beast". It seemed almost daily there were reports of new sightings of the "beast" or the discovery of more animals that had been killed by some mysterious creature.

District and national news organizations picked up the story and soon Bladenboro was overwhelmed with hunters eager to find the beast. One report said 600 hunters came all the way from Tennessee. Another report stated a fully armed pack of fraternity brothers from UNC- Chapel Hill came to help free the town of the terrifying creature. The report wasn't clear as to what they were armed with.

Eventually, there were no new sightings of the beast and no new killings of dogs or hogs, etc. A story began to circulate that the Mayor of Bladenboro, Mayor Bob Fussell, may have started or at least fueled the flames. He owned the theatre in town and in the midst of the furor had booked the movie "*The Big Cat*". He had put up big advertising posters about the movie with the wording: "Now you can see the Cat! We've got him on our screen! And in Technicolor!" Due to the story and to the advertising, the movie was sold out at almost every showing.

Gradually, the attention of Wilmington turned to more interesting events such as the story about fourteen year old Wentworth Jamieson who got a new bike for Christmas. As he was riding his bike along the waterfront near the foot of Chestnut Street while looking for some friends, he wasn't looking where he was going and suddenly realized he was about to run off the dock into the river.

He stomped on the brake pedal but forgot the brakes on his new bike were on the handlebars. He sailed off into the Cape Fear River. He could swim and was able to save himself but his bike sank into about thirty feet of water. Fortunately for him, a couple of men, Curley Bryant and James Teachey, who were working in the nearby garage of the Star-News Newspapers, were able to fashion a grappling hook out of cable wire and retrieved his bike. So Wentworth was able to ride his new bike back home albeit in wet, cold clothing.

One of the sports at NHHS seldom mentioned in the papers, in Teen Age Tattler or Teen Scene was the ROTC rifle team. Competition for the team was held in January, 1954. Fifteen cadets were selected based on their skill in shooting the thirty caliber rifle in the firing range located in the basement of the Isaac Bear Building. They were J. E. Carrol, Roland Register, Rolin Harrell, Alex Thompson, David Millinor, David Bennett, William Hanchey, Alva Ward, Jere Danford, Ed Dye, Ronald Baldwin, Donald Fountain, Andrew Canoutas, David Rooks and Alva Stanland.

In a match with the Cape Fear Rifle Club, the NHHS R. O. T. C. tem won by a score of 1, 627 points to 654. Leading the NHHS teas was David Millinor with 346 points and David Rooks close behind with 337.

An exciting announcement was made in January, 1954, by Mr. Hugh MacRae II that his real estate development company, The Oleander Company, was about to begin construction of a large shopping center on Oleander Drive just east of the city limits.

It would be named the Hanover Shopping Center. The building would be entirely air conditioned and have a big super-market, a variety store, a drug store and other conveniences and service shops as well as branch bank facilities. Mr. MacRae expected the Hanover Shopping Center to be in full operation by early 1955.

I was now working at Futrelle's Pharmacy and had my nights free. So I was able to play basketball in the City League at the Community Center. In the first game in 1954, my team, the Wolverines, beat our opponent, the Blue Eagles, by a score of 73-18. I had a good night scoring 27 points.

The Azalea Festival Committee was beginning to make announcements about events and celebrities that would be appearing at the 1954 Azalea Festival. The first event would be a Pre-Azalea Festival Dance to take place on February 22 at the Moose Temple. The music for the dance was to be provided by Ralph Marterie and his Downbeat Orchestra. He and his band had two top ten hits in 1953, *Pretend* and *Caravan.*

Tickets purchased in advance were set at $2.00 each but cost $2.25 at the door.

Even more exciting than the appearance of Ralph Marterie and The Downbeats was the announcement Big Jon and Sparky were to be here for the Festival. Every NHHS student, as a child, had listened to their show on WMFD radio. Big Jon and Sparky were scheduled to give two performances at

NHHS on Friday afternoon, March 26, and another that night. There would also be two more shows at NHHS on Saturday afternoon and Saturday night.

At the Wilmington Open Table Tennis Tournament held at the Community Center, several NHHS students showed their ping-pong skills. Bonnie Shain won the Men's Singles event as well as the Junior Boy's Singles; Gary Preston and Bonnie Shain won the Men's Doubles event; Dr. Van Velsor and Martina Lipsey won the Mixed Doubles event; Ann Chadwick won the Women's Singles and Martina Lipsey came in second; and in the Women's Doubles event, Gretchen Thomas and Ann Chadwick won while Martina Lipsey and Catherine Sumner came in second.

As busy as they were, some NHHS students managed to find time to model clothing at a fashion show at the Community Center put on by the Teen-Age Division of the Seventh Annual Azalea Festival. Modeling dresses and coats were Margaret Rowe, Barbara Austin, Jane Bellamy, Sandra Kalfin, Sally Johnson and Nancy Futch. Modeling young men's fashions provided by Ed Fleishman and Brothers were Charles Wade, David Bennett, Raiford Trask, Tommy Capps, Bob Godley and Bobbie Johnson.

Chapter 35

A Real TV Remote Controller

WMFD-TV began broadcasting on April 1, 1954. In 1958, the station changed its name to WECT-TV. The station was located on the second floor in the same building as WMFD radio on Princess Street between Second and Third.

In its pioneer days, almost all of its shows were local productions. This was the typical schedule every day with the exception of Friday and Saturday:

4-6 PM	Test Pattern
6:630PM	Over At Al's
6:30-6:45 PM	Evening Edition News
6:45-7:00 PM	Weather
7:00-8:00 PM	Western Theater
8:00-8:30 PM	To Be Announced

8:30-9:00 PM	TV Song Shop
9:00-9:05 PM	News Capsule
9:05-10:30PM	Late Show
10:30 PM	Sign Off

On Friday evenings, we could watch *The Life of Riley* and on Saturday evenings, we could watch *The Hit Parade*. Both of these shows were recordings of old shows.

With an outside antenna and if the weather was right, WNCT-TV in Greenville could be seen. This required an outside antenna which had to be rotated to the correct angle so the signal could be received. The Greenville station had some really good shows; *Perry Como, I Love Lucy, Ozzie and Harriett,* and *Red Skelton.*

The City of Wilmington City Council had the foresight to write regulations that covered the installation of outside antennas. *"No antennas are to be mounted on chimneys that are not in good condition and must have flue linings extending to their tops. Specified chimney mounts must be used and the mast assembly shall not exceed 10 feet in overall height above the top of the chimney.*

All masts and hardware must be of a non-corrosive material or coating, and approved brackets must be used where the antennas are attached directly to the building. Each 10 feet of mast must have at least three properly spaced guy wires."

Beginning in February, several stores in Wilmington began to place ads in the newspaper that displayed the various TV sets they had for sell. Hughes Bros. offered a large Firestone floor model TV for $463.50, Barefoots & Jackson had a table Bendix model for $183.50, while MacMillan and Cameron had what Mother thought was the best deal, a 21 inch table model with HaloLight for $199.95. As Mother had a charge account at MacMillan and Cameron Co., she decided to buy a set there where she could make monthly payments of $10.00.

Gerald, Coleman and I were overjoyed at this unexpected luxury. Since I had first seen a TV in Billie Brinkley's store in Chinquapin, I had dreamed of having one in our home but never really expected it to happen.

We quickly found our only viewing choice was WECT-TV which offered limited watching opportunities. We got tired quickly of watching *Over At Al's* and *Western Theater*. I did enjoy Hayseed's comedy routines when he appeared with the Silver Star Quartet. After listening to friends talk about the wonderful programs available from WNCT-TV, I made plans to get an outside antenna

I told Mother I would pay for an outside antenna from my earnings at Futrelle's Pharmacy if she would agree to let me do that. She did and I bought the cheapest one that MacMillan and Cameron had.

I didn't know the City of Wilmington had regulations governing the installation of outside antennas so in my installation, I violated all the regulations that had ever been written; no brackets, no guy wires, just a strand of baling wire wrapped around the antenna base and around the chimney. I thought I did a pretty good job.

It was true we could get a signal from the Greenville station provided the antenna was turned in the correct direction, which was in a different direction from which the WECT signal was received. Whenever we wanted to watch another channel, I would have to go upstairs, out onto the small back porch, climb up a post, hoist myself onto the roof and walk over to the chimney and rotate the antenna by hand.

Gerald would stand in the living room where the TV set was located and watch the screen. If the signal wasn't as good as it should have been, he would yell to Coleman who stood on the front porch the antenna needed to be turned a few degrees to the left. In turn, Coleman would yell up to me Gerald's instructions. Accordingly, I would turn the antenna as Gerald directed and wait for follow-up instructions. If the TV picture wasn't good enough, the procedure would be repeated until we got it right. It may have taken five or six adjustments to get the best reception.

Our technique for changing TV channels may have been the first "remote control,"

In addition to TV, many people got their entertainment from reading the daily comics in the Wilmington Star-News and the Wilmington Evening News.

The Wilmington Star-News conducted another survey in March, 1954, which asked its reader to vote for their favorite comic strip. When I read the results, I was really disappointed; my favorite "*The Phantom*" had fallen from first place a year earlier to third place this year, behind "*Rex Morgan*" and "*Mary Worth*," two comic strips that weren't even in the top ten in 1953.

The Rex Morgan comic strip was about a family physician, who was compassionate, socially-conscious and personally invested in his patients' best interests.

Mary Worth was a compassionate widow, living in a condominium complex, who befriended and advised friends, neighbors and acquaintances. In other words, she was a very nosy busybody who was always in the middle of somebody's business and telling them what they should do.

How anybody would prefer an incompetent doctor and a nosy widow to the Phantom was more than I could understand. It just went to show how unappreciative of story plots comic strip readers were.

Chapter 36
My Social Life at NHHS

I didn't have much of a social life at NHHS. By nature, I was somewhat shy. Growing up in the small farming community of Chinquapin didn't help much. The social skills I had learned there for the first fourteen years of my life didn't equip me to feel comfortable with most other students at NHHS who had lived all their lives in the city.

About the only social I attended during my high school years, other than the ones that took place on school grounds, was a wiener roast at Silver Lake one Saturday. Grier White and I had spent Friday night with Stanley Thompson who lived just down Carolina Beach Road from its intersection with Silver Lake Road.

The three of us walked over to Silver Lake Saturday afternoon just as other friends were beginning to arrive in their cars. After the cookout, the boys played some dodge ball, threw some footballs while the girls sat around and talked. The games made some of us pretty warm. We had worn bathing trunks under our clothes in the event an opportunity for swimming arose.

Grier White and I were eager to display our swimming skills before such a distinguished group. We and a few others jumped into the lake and started showing off. As Grier and I were on the swimming team, we began swimming circles around the other boys. They soon had enough and went ashore while I continued demonstrating all the swimming styles: the freestyle, the backstroke, the breast stroke, and the butterfly.

After a demonstration of each stroke during which I exhausted myself, I realized no one was looking at me. They were busy talking. I crawled up on the shore and threw up as I often did after finishing a swimming event. I then realized everyone was looking at me. I raked some sand over the mess. Stanley wrote on a piece of cardboard and placed it over the mess, "Beware of the vomit". He was thoughtful that way.

I seldom, if ever, thought about dating. In addition to being shy, I had one other major drawback. I had no driver's license and even if I had one, I didn't have access to a car. It was important to have a car if you wanted to ask a girl for a date.

Many of my classmates had cars; beautiful cars, in fact. Tommy Millard had a 1941 Cadillac convertible. Other classmates were given cars by their parents on their 16th or 17th birthdays. In one of the Teen Age Tattler columns, written by Patsy Barrett, she named several students who were frequently seen cruising around the school area in their fancy cars during lunch hour or after school.

When Tommy rode by in his Cadillac convertible, many of the girls would smile and wave, perhaps hoping to get a ride with him.

My friend, Vernon Meshaw, got his driver's license during his senior year at NHHS. As noted earlier, Vernon's Daddy and older brother were in the junk business. His Daddy had a huge truck that was large enough to haul a lot of junk. When the cab was disconnected from the trailer, it made for a comfortable ride although it was an unusually large vehicle.

Vernon occasionally got permission to drive the truck cab to school. He would pick me up and off we would ride to NHHS. He had to park on Dock Street somewhere between

10th and 11 Streets in order to find a parking space that would accommodate such a large vehicle.

Vernon and I decided one afternoon after school we would cruise around the school in his truck. As we rode by the front of the school on Market Street, Vernon blew the horn, trying to get the attention of several girls standing around on the sidewalk. When we saw some of the girls waving we were encouraged but then we realized they were not waving at us but waving to get the exhaust smoke away from their face. We didn't cruise around the school any more.

According to the Teen Age Tattler, written by Patsy Barrett, and Teen Times, written by Edith Darden, the great majority of seniors were continually going to parties or dances at White's Lodge, the Edgewater Club or the Community Center. Of those three places, the only I one knew was the Community Center. I didn't even know where the other two places were located. I spent a lot of time at the Community Center playing ping-pong or basketball but never did any dancing there.

Dancing was an accomplishment that was beyond my ability to learn. My experience with dancing in the Girls' Gym in the Isaac Bear Building while I was a freshman had scarred me forever. I had absolutely no sense of rhythm and felt everyone was laughing and pointing at me when I attempted to dance.

As the date of the annual TWIRP dance approached, I was half afraid and half hoping some girl would ask me to go with her. As I didn't have a car, it would have to be a girl that had her own car who could pick me up and take me back home after the dance.

One afternoon while in Mrs. Hovis' English class, Mimi Bergen, who sat across the aisle from me, whispered, "I want to ask you something after class. Stick around, okay?" Although I was elated, I spent the remainder of the class thinking up some good excuses for not being able to go with her to the TWIRP dance: Mr. Futrelle needed me to stay late on Saturday and make a lot of chicken salad; our outside TV antenna had fallen over and Mother wanted me to put it back up after finishing work at Futrelle's on the day of the dance; the First Baptist Church had scheduled Youth Sunday a week after the dance, and wanted all participants to meet on the night of the dance to prepare and I believed I was going to be asked to be the Youth Minister, etc. I thought the chicken salad excuse was probably the most plausible one.

After class, Mimi leaned over and asked, "You work at Futrelle's with Jimmy Forrester, don't you? Has he said anything about being asked to the TWIRP dance? I want to ask him but I want to know if he's still available."

I went from elation to deflation quickly. "I'm not sure," I said. "He may have to stay late at Futrelle's on that Saturday to make up some chicken salad. I haven't heard him say about being asked to the dance,"

When the last school dance of the year, the Junior-Senior Prom, drew closer, I resolved to ask a girl to go with me to the dance. Before I could ask someone, I had to arrange transportation. Luckily, Jimmy Covil, who had worked with me as an usher at the Baily Theatre at one time, invited me and my date, if I could get one, to ride with him and his date, Ann Croom.

I was undecided as to whom I should ask. Although I had stepped on the feet of several girls during our dancing classes in my freshman year during P. E. class under the supervision of Mrs. Tillet, I didn't think I knew them well enough to ask them to go with me to the prom. Eula Craft was the only one who wasn't taller than me as well as the only one whose feet I hadn't stepped on too badly. I had even managed to carry on a conversation with her although she hadn't been very interested in Collard Stealing Night.

As she was in my homeroom my senior year, Room 311, I spoke to her almost every day but asking a girl for a date was much different than talking about collard stealing. One morning I told myself "Get this behind you," so I stammered out my invitation. To my surprise and relief, she said she would be happy to go with me. I couldn't believe it had been that easy after struggling to get up enough nerve to ask for several days.

When the afternoon of the Prom arrived on Saturday, May 15, 1954, I began to get even more nervous than when I asked Eula to go with me. What should I wear? What should we talk about? Should I try to dance? Suppose I get sick and throw up? Dancing was as exhausting as swimming and a lot more stressful.

Jimmy and Ann came by my house and I crawled into the back seat. Ann looked beautiful in her prom dress. Jimmy didn't look so hot; his hair wasn't coiffured exactly right but neither was mine. I may have used a little too much Brylcreem. I didn't know his hair tonic of choice.

When we arrived at Eula's house, I slowly got out of the car, walked to the front door and rang the doorbell. Eula opened the door. I couldn't believe how beautiful she looked, prettier than Ann, I thought.

When we arrived at the gym, we couldn't find a close-by parking space. Jimmy told me to get out with the girls and he would go somewhere and park and walk back to the gym. I quietly begged him not to leave me alone with the two girls. He agreed to let me ride with him to a parking space while Ann and Eula waited inside the gym.

They were waiting for us just inside the gym door. The gym was already full of couples; some were sitting while others were standing around talking. I found a table that had two empty chairs and Eula and I sat down while Jimmy and Ann wandered off to find some of their close friends.

The only two times I left my seat was to get some food for Eula and myself and to dance the one dance I felt somewhat comfortable doing, the Bunny Hop. Even though the Bunny Hop was a simple dance, I somehow managed to get out of step. I was hipping when I should have been hopping. I just knew other classmates were laughing and pointing at me.

As Eula and I sat at our table during the long hours of the Prom, some friends came by and talked with us. I was so glad to welcome them to our table, even for a short while. If Eula and I were by ourselves, I found it extremely difficult to make interesting conversation. However, I had a plan. Before I left my house, I had made a list of conversation topics I thought may be of interest to Eula and others. I put the list in my coat pocket in the event I would need it to stimulate conversation.

I needed it several times. On the list, I had jotted down: Macao Light, Baily Theatre experiences, making chicken salad sandwiches, TV remote controllers, Dry Pond life, my family ran away from home, swim team events and throwing up, what I hoped to be when I grew up, Charles Laughton, and a few others. I didn't put down Collard Stealing Night because I had covered that topic during our dancing lessons in our freshman year and didn't need to bring that up again.

Eula was very gracious. She had to carry the brunt of the conversation; talking about her teachers, her classes, her hopes of going to college, her close friends, her church, her shoes and her clothing, cooking, her hair-do's, etc.. I saw Jimmy and Ann whirl by every so often.

Finally, the Prom was over. I apologized to Eula for being such a bore. She assured me it was okay and she had enjoyed the evening. When I walked her back to her front door and her parents let her in, they asked her if she had had a good time. I believed she told a fib when she said she did.

Jimmy and Ann dropped me off at my house and took off. They had made arrangements to meet some of their close friends at a party after the Prom. I was glad I didn't have to go. Four hours of partying were enough for me for one evening. That was my only date during my years at NHHS.

Chapter 37
I Discover I'm Not a Writer

My English teacher for my final semester at NHHS was Mrs. Doris Hovis. She was an excellent teacher and made learning the intricacies of the English language bearable, even dangling participles and the pluperfect tense became somewhat understandable.

However, as the semester neared an end she made an assignment which caused me a lot of stress. She told us we were to write a short story that had to be at least 2,500 words in length.

I was never good at making projects teachers required to demonstrate we had learned something in their class that semester. I generally tried to make something out of Paper Mache. Mother was not happy to see me begin a Paper Mache project. My formula of flour, water and torn strips of newspaper didn't always come out in the right consistency. The pot I used required a lot of scrubbing after the paste was made.

In French II, when Mr. Browning told us we had to make a project with a French theme before the end of the semester, I felt as if a heavy black cloud had descended on me. I thought and thought, and thought some more, as to what I could make with a French theme. I pulled an encyclopedia from a shelf in the library and scanned through the pages about France. My eyes fell on the Eiffel Tower. I can make one of those I said to myself. All I'll need is a lot of popsicle sticks painted black, a knife and some glue. After several hours of painting, trimming and gluing, I had created a bad image of something that resembled the Fire Tower in Mill Swamp after a hurricane.

After I tossed the Eiffel Tower in the trash, I went back to the encyclopedia. The Arc de Triomphe caught my eye. The obvious medium needed to build an Arc de Triomphe was Paper Mache, a medium that generally didn't work for me. However, all I needed was two columns and a crosspiece across the top of the columns. I can make one of those I said to myself.

I was wrong. After several hours of work with flour, water and newspaper, my Arc De Triomphe collapsed into a pile of wet trash. I went back to the encyclopedia. The Notre Dame Cathedral caught my eye.

I thought I would only build the main building without the wings, the annexes, and the flying buttresses. Surely, Mr. Browning would reward me for my effort. I had some valuable experience in constructing small wooden structures; building bird houses in Bible School. After several hours of work with small strips of wood, a knife, hammer and nails, I had made what resembled a bird house but not quite. I had been unable to put a pitch on the roof and it was almost flat.

As I was out of time, I had to go with Notre Dame. After painting it with appropriate colors, I carried it into the classroom on the last day. Mr. Browning looked at it curiously and asked me, "What's that supposed to be?"

I hesitantly answered, "What do you think it is?"

He replied, "Well, it sort of looks like a bird house but even more like a chicken house. Where's the French theme? Oh, wait, I think I see. You've made a chicken house for the three French Hens. Very clever."

I didn't appreciate his sense of humor. Because he had a good laugh at my French project, he was more generous with the grade he gave to me than I deserved.

Sometimes these projects near the end of the semester caused me to have nightmares. The one I had repeatedly was a situation where the final exam for a particular class was to be taken that day and I hadn't been to a class in several weeks. I couldn't even remember where the exam classroom was. I wondered up and down the hallways at NHHS hoping to see a classmate that would call me into the exam room. Another part of the dream was I needed my text book but couldn't find my locker. I couldn't remember which floor it was on or what end of the building. I was so glad to wake up and find it was all a dream.

In my teen-age years, I dreamed a lot. I dreamed of being a professional basketball player, captain of a U. S. Navy submarine, a movie star in cowboy western movies, etc. Some of them were so realistic, I wrote down the gist of the dreams when I woke up. As I looked through my gists, one seemed to be something I could possibly turn into a short story with some creative writing.

One night I dreamed a Broadway show was having try-outs for a male lead role in a musical. Some friends and family members encouraged me to try out. The try-outs were held after hours in Efird's Department Store.

Debbie Fisher was in charge of the try-outs. In my dream, I sang and danced a duet with her. While opening and closing an umbrella, I was leaping up on the counters and then over to another counter, down to the floor and back up on a counter, all in perfect time to "*Singing In The Rain,*" sung by Gene Kelly. Meanwhile, the change canisters were whizzing back and forth throughout the store in perfect time with the music.

Also, I was singing along with Gene and Debbie. Although my dancing was perfect, I could tell my singing needed some work. I just knew Debbie would select me. Just as we were finishing the piece, Mr. Sam Taylor, the music director at NHHS, and Mrs. Jean Tillit, the girls' PE teacher, stepped in, laughed, and pointed at me. The music stopped and I woke up. I was so disappointed when I awoke. I desperately wanted to know if Debbie selected me.

The fact that I had seen *Singing in the Rain* almost twenty times while I was an usher at the Baily Theatre may have caused me to have such a dream.

I tried three times to make a short story out of this dream but just couldn't make it work.

I thought and pondered what I could write about in my short story for Mrs. Hovis. It kept me awake at night. I didn't have much of an imagination and the topics that came to my mind would have been impossible about which to write 2,500 words. Mimi Bergen sat next to me in the class and we shared our thoughts about possible topics.

She asked me about several topics she had in mind. Many of them reminded me of some *"Mary Worth"* episodes I had read in the comic strips. I wondered if she was one of the thousands of comic strip readers who had voted *"Mary Worth"* as the most popular comic strip. I asked her why she didn't write a story about the Phantom but she didn't like his skin tight outfit or his mask that completely covered his entire head.

After several attempts, I settled on writing about a quarterback who on the final play of the game threw a touchdown pass to the tight end. It was a miracle play the way I described it. The quarterback had struggled all year and his team had lost several important games through no fault of his own; dropped passes, fumbles, penalties, etc. had caused his team to suffer defeat after defeat. But in the final game, he executed beautifully, escaped several would-be tacklers and completed a 50 yard pass into the end zone. What an ending! I was glad Jimmy Williams wasn't in my class.[12] Mrs. Hovis gave me a B minus.

Much of the story consisted of a description of the weather, the football stadium, the ugly uniforms of the opponents' team, the antics of the cheerleaders, etc., anything to make up the required 2,500 words.

The day after we all turned in out short stories, Mrs. Hovis called three students to the front of the room to read their short

---

[12] Jimmy Williams was quarterback for the NHHS football team. He was appointed to attend the U.S. Naval Academy and eventually attained the rank of Admiral in the Navy.

stories. She told us their stories were the epitome of short story writing and we would appreciate the effort these three students had put into their writing.

Much to my surprise Vernon Meshaw was one of the three students so honored. I had never suspected he had any writing talent but you can't always tell a book by its cover.

But when Vernon began reading his short story, I began to suspect that maybe; just maybe, he had "borrowed" some parts of his story. He was using words I knew were never in his vocabulary; words like "staccato" and "filigrade" and "anonymous,"

After class when I asked him about his creative story, he told me he had put off writing his story until the night before it was due. He had no idea what to write about so he resorted to borrowing a short story from a comic book "G. I. Joe," In addition to the comic strips in the book, there was a short story in the middle of the book about an attack on German lines during World War II.

Vernon believed, rightfully so, neither Mrs. Hovis nor any of our classmates would be reading a short story from the comic book "G. I. Joe," He got away with it. The grade he received on his short story raised his overall semester grade to a C minus.

That episode convinced me I was not a writer. I made a vow I would never try write anything again other than book reports, a research theme or an essay.

Chapter 38
My First and Last Political Campaign

So that NHHS students would be exposed to the ins and outs of political campaigning as well as learn how different levels of city and county government worked, elections were held each May in which students were encouraged to run for an elective office of their choice. The elected students held their office for one day and under the supervision of the real elected officials, conducted the business of the office to which they were elected.

The different positions that students could campaign for were: County Commissioners, County Sheriff, County

Auditor, Recorder's Court Judge, County Solicitor, Clerk of Superior Court, City Council, and many others. These elected officials also made appointments of other students to city and county administrative positions for a day.

I had no thought of running for an office until a few days before the election, which took place on May 7, 1954, Katherine Graham told me I should run for the office of County Commissioner and she would be my campaign manager. I was always so in awe of Katherine I naturally agreed to her suggestion without further thought. I would have done anything she asked of me, with the exception of dancing.

. When I saw the other candidates for County Commissioner, I told Katherine I should just immediately withdraw because I would have no chance of winning an election against such popular and outstanding students.

She sat down with me and we read over the list: Arthur Jordan, Jimmy Covil, Richard Buck, Bill Tilley, Pennie Petros, Pat Swart, Bob Buck, Buddy Harrelson, Nancy Bates, Carl Dempsey, Charlene Ray, Charles Martin, Glenda Clewis, Alan Croom, Sally Ottaway, Jerry Smith, Robert Murphy, Howard Stampley, Girffin Hamilton, and David Checkner.

"Why, Kenan," she said "there's no one on that list any more popular than you. Besides, with me as your campaign manager you may get a lot of votes just because I ask. Who do you think knows more students than I do?"

"Well," I answered. "There's Patsy Barrett, and uh, Betty Bordeaux, and uh, Karen Kurka, and maybe Gloria Smith. They're not more popular but they're up there at the top."

"You're right," Katherine responded. "But I believe I can get them to support you and if they support you, their friends are likely to help us out."

Katherine was a smooth-talking campaign manager. She seemed to be an old hand at politicking. Posters began appearing around the school with a slogan she thought of: "Maready is Ready," "Others are only half-ready".

Other slogans didn't compare: "The Buck Stops Here"; "Let a Ray Shine In"; "Buddy, Can You Spare A Vote": "Don't be Silly, Vote For Tilley".

On May 4 and May 5, at two assemblies for government classes only, the candidates were introduced by their campaign managers to the audience. The candidates then gave a short speech setting forth all the reasons why they should be elected.

In her introduction of me, Katherine built me up so much, I thought before she mentioned my name she was about to introduce some other candidate. When I walked up to address the students, I forgot everything I was going to say. Finally, I stammered out "Like Katherine said, vote for me. Thank you."

I think the students appreciated my very short speech. They were beginning to get restless as they had already heard a lot of oratory. They gave me a great ovation as I went back to my seat.

On Thursday, May 7, all students in the government classes were given rather lengthy ballots. The ballots were counted that day and on the next morning the wining candidates were announced. I was really surprised to learn I had been elected to be one of the five County Commissioners for a day. Katherine's prowess as a campaign manager had won the day for me.

During the day, as other students congratulated me, a horrible thought came to my mind. As soon as I could, I located Katherine and expressed my concern: "Katherine, it seems to me every time our school has some event, somebody wants to hold a dance to celebrate. I'm afraid if that happens, I'm going to be asked to lead off the dance. I really don't want to dance as a County Commissioner. I know everybody will be laughing and pointing at me,"

Katherine assured me, as far as she knew, nobody was planning a dance to celebrate the elections. I breathed a sigh of relief.

On Thursday, May 13, all city and county offices were taken over by a swarm of NHHS students. It seemed about half the student body was running around those offices. The City Council students and the County Commissioner students were required to appoint other students to fill all the administrative, judicial, law enforcement, parks and recreation, etc., positions.

I used my County Commissioner appointing power to appoint Vernon as county tax collector, a position he really enjoyed. It got him out of school for a day.

The students who were elected to serve as County Commissioners were: Allen Croom, Chairman, Carl Dempsey, Tex Jordan, David Checkner and me. Students elected to serve on the City Council were Jimmy Williams, mayor, David Barefoot, Don Frost, Murle Teachey, and Tommy Capps.

In those days, women were pretty much overlooked when it came to running for office, even among high school students. Out of seventeen elected positions, only two girls were elected: Betty Bordeaux as County Auditor and Mary Nell Piver as Recorder's Court Judge. But they did make good campaign managers.

On the front page of the Wilmington Morning Star, May 14, 1954, there was an article about the meeting of the student Commissioners and the actions that were discussed and taken by the Board. On Page 2 there was a picture of participants in the meeting with real Commissioners Ralph Horton and Thurston Watkins in attendance. I was amazed to see my picture in the paper. I hoped my old friends in Chinquapin would see the article.

Unfortunately, for some reason, Tex Jordan and I were badly blurred in the picture. If I hadn't known who I was, I wouldn't have known who I was.

Chapter 39
Graduation at Last

Nothing noteworthy happened the rest of the school year after my day of serving my community as County Commissioner for a day. After we finished our final exams, the only major thing left to do was to graduate. That ceremony took place at Legion Stadium on the night of Friday, May 28, 1954. Three hundred and sixty-six boys and girls left their high school days behind and looked forward to their future.

Many of my classmates had definite plans for their future. Our class president, Bob Godley, announced at our graduation that 107 students planned to go into business administration, another 119 planned to enter different professions, including 48 who planned to study medicine, while twelve hoped to be salesmen and 28 wanted to be teachers.

Senior Class Picture 1954

That left approximately 125 who either didn't know or wouldn't say what they wanted to be when they grew up, including me. My priority was to get a job as soon as possible. I had no thoughts of going to college.

However, when I read an article in the Wilmington Star News about teachers' pay in New Hanover County schools, I wished I could get a college education. I didn't know that teachers were so highly paid. The Chairman of the Board of Education, Dr. John T. Hoggard, provided some information to the paper about teachers' pay and benefits.

According to Dr. Hoggard, a beginning teacher was paid $270 a month for nine months. On a twelve month basis, this averaged out to be $213.37 a month. After teaching for eleven years, a teacher reached the maximum monthly salary of $380 for nine months, which resulted in a twelve month average of $285.00. To this salary paid by the state, New Hanover County paid a supplement of $20 a month and if the teacher had a graduate degree, the monthly supplement was increased to $23.50.

However, teachers got no sick leave and if they were absent due to illness, seven dollars a day were deducted to pay their substitute. If they were absent due to personal or business reasons, the whole day's salary was deducted from their pay.

A monthly salary of $270, to me, would have been a dream come true. I thought if I could ever make half that much, or $35 a week, I would think myself well-off.

The biggest obstacle to my getting a well-paying job was my utter lack of marketable skills. During my working life, I had cropped tobacco, picked beans, ushered at a theatre and worked as a soda-jerk. None of those professions qualified me for much of anything.

In my final year at NHHS, I had taken a typing class under Miss Julia Bray and a bookkeeping course under Mrs. Mary Hood. Miss Bray told me I was an excellent typist, typing around 65 to 70 words per minute. She gave me an A. And I had enjoyed the bookkeeping course taught by Mrs. Hood. She also gave me an A.

Prior to graduation, I had called upon a few businesses in the area to apply for a job. It seemed no one needed a young man who could type 70 words per minute or knew the difference between a debit and a credit or could reconcile a bank account.

On Monday morning, May 31, 1954, I began looking for a job in earnest. Babcock and Wilcox didn't need me, neither did the Atlantic Coastline Railroad Company or any of the other large businesses in the area. I lowered my sights and began applying at retail stores with the same result. My final list of possible employers included the shoe stores.

There were eleven shoe stores in Wilmington on Front Street at the time: Shoe Mart, 16 S. Front; Freeman Shoe Co., 24 N. Front, Kinney Shoes, 30 N. Front; Thom McAnn, 32 N. Front; Merit Shoe Co., 112 N. Front; Su-Ann Shoe Store, 121 N. Front; Cinderella Booterie, 127 N. Front; Salby Shoe

Salon, 141 N. Front; Butler's Shoe Store, 155 N. Front; Cannon's Shoe Co., 201 N. Front; and Stanaland's Shoe Store, 409 N. Front St.

I just knew one of those eleven shoe stores would need a top-notch shoe salesman. In preparation for my applications at the stores, I bought a new pair of shoes from Efird's Dept. Store so the managers would see the importance I placed on being well shoed.

Something went wrong. I believe the store managers saw right away I didn't have my heart in becoming a shoe salesman. Or it could have been they saw I had not purchased my new shoes from their store.

I was still only seventeen years of age and looked even younger than that. My potential employers may have thought I was too immature to be a reliable employee.

In June, I had run out of options with respect to getting a job in Wilmington so I decided I would look in a much larger city. My sister, Sudie, was then living in Winston-Salem with her husband and two small daughters.

I said goodbye to Mother, Gerald, Coleman, and a few of my close friends. I told them I would probably not be back in Wilmington until the Christmas holidays. I also, in jest, asked Mother not to move while I was gone without telling me.

I walked downtown to the Greyhound Bus Station at Second and Walnut Streets, bought a one-way ticket to Winston-Salem and off I went. I was back in three weeks still without a job.

My success at getting employment in Winston-Salem was the same as that in Wilmington. I had applied at dozens of businesses during the three weeks but to no avail. The closest I came to getting a job was at McLean Trucking Co. I filled in their application and took some sort of IQ test. I was told I did so well on the test I was over qualified to fill any jobs that were available at McLean's at the present time. I was too smart for my own good.

Chapter 40
S. H. Kress & Co.

I was relieved to find Mother hadn't moved while I was in Winston-Salem. My family was still living at 10 ½ South Seventh Street. The night I got back I called my friend, Vernon Meshaw. After graduation, he opted not to join his father and older brother in the scrap iron business.

Instead, he was able to get a job working in the stockroom at S. H. Kress & Co., one of the four or five largest Five and Dime store chains in the country. He intended to stay with S. H. Kress and gradually work his way up to a management position. Vernon told me there was a vacancy in the stockroom and I should apply for a job there.

At that time there were five Five and Dime stores in Wilmington, four of them on North Front Street: S. H. Kress & Co., at 11 N. Front St; McLelland Stores at 23 N. Front; F. W. Woolworth Co., at 122 N. Front; and H. L. Green Co., at 254 N. Front Street. A locally owned Five and Dime Store, Goldings, was at 1602 Market St.

The very next day I went to the Kress store, applied for a job and was hired immediately. I was ecstatic. I could hardly wait to tell Mother I had a real job paying $35 a week for only forty-eight hours work. The store was open for business from nine a.m. until 5:30 p.m. every day, Monday through Saturday. She and I sat down that night and prepared a new budget based on our increased income. It was amazing what an extra $30 a week could buy, the amount I got after Social Security and income tax deductions.

Working in the stockroom was fairly simple but physically wearing. Trucks came in daily with loads of boxes of merchandise that had to be unpacked and the contents put on shelves in the stockrooms. The girls who worked at the various retail counters on the sales floor would prepare a list of the items they needed each day to replenish their counter. Vernon and I would pick up the lists, go into the stockrooms, and pull the requested items from the shelves, put them into a basket and pull the baskets to the counters.

There was never any time when there was not something to do. The empty cardboard boxes and other packing material had to be baled. There was a huge baling machine in the basement stockroom into which the boxes and packing material was tossed. Once the container was filled, the machine was activated and a heavy metal lid would press the materials down into the container. This process was repeated until the container could hold no more stuff. Baling wires were wrapped around the paper bales and with the use of hand trucks, the bales were placed outside in the alley awaiting pickup by the waste paper company.

The company that picked up the bales of paper was Wilmington Paper Stock Co. It was a family business owned by the father of one of my classmates, Bobby Warwick.

One day in order to test my strength, I stood on a front flange of the baling machine and tried to hold back the heavy lid as it came down. Just in time, the thought occurred to me I may not have enough strength to hold back the lid and if I didn't, my arms were about to be caught by the lid and torn off my shoulders. A little skin was scraped off my arms as I pulled them out but it could have been much worse. A double amputee would find it difficult to find employment, certainly not at S. H. Kress & Co., as a stock boy.

After I had worked a couple of months, I began to dream of getting my driver's license and a car of my own. Mother thought that would be a waste of money. As we lived at 10 ½ South Seventh Street, it was only a seven block walk to Kress's. My argument for buying a car was we could visit her old friends and relatives in Chinquapin on Sundays, and I was beginning to think about dating. She finally agreed and I began looking at ads in the newspaper.

But first, I had to get my driver's license. I certainly didn't want to own a car and have no license to drive. I studied the manual for a few days and asked Daddy to take me to the examining station. I passed the vision test and the paper test with flying colors. The driving test was going okay but on our return trip there was a stop sign at the top of a hill.

Stopping on a hill while driving a straight shift car is a tricky business, at least it was for me. Operation of the clutch, the brake and the accelerator has to be synchronized or bad things happen. With only two feet and three pedals to operate,

I couldn't always decide which pedal needed to be pushed and which to be released.

As I came to a stop at the stop sign, I pushed in the clutch and pressed the accelerator. My car began rolling back down the hill. "Use the brake!! Use the brake," the examiner yelled.

I took my foot off the accelerator, pressed down on the brake, released the clutch, and the engine cut off. Rather than trying to start the engine while on the hill, and despite the examiner's instructions, I let the car roll backwards until we came to the bottom of the hill.

"Can I try that again'? I asked. "I think I know what I did wrong." "Just about everything you did was wrong," the examiner retorted. "But I'll give you one more chance."

I got the engine started, put the car in low gear and drove slowly up the hill. As I approached the stop sign, I got confused again. I pressed the accelerator and let out the clutch. We shot across the intersection barely missing a big fertilizer truck coming out of the Heide Warehouse Company yard.

The examining station was just across the intersection and I was able to come to a jerking halt right in front. We went into the office and the examiner told me, "You'd be a menace to the driving public. Didn't you take Drivers Ed at school?"

"No, sir," I replied. "I thought it would be a waste of time as I already knew how to drive."

"I don't know how you got that idea," he said. "Come back again when you've learned how to stop a car at the top of a hill. And make sure you don't get me as your examiner."

Vernon had a Hudson with automatic drive and he let me practice with it a few times late in the afternoons at the examining station with particular attention given to the stop sign at the top of the hill. With a car with an automatic transmission, I had no trouble passing the next time I tried. I was careful not to get the angry examiner.

With my driver's license now in my wallet, I was ready to buy a car. After some diligent research, I saw someone wanted to sell their 1949 Ford for $250. According to the ad, the car was in excellent condition and had been only driven by a little old lady who drove it to church on Sundays. It looked as if some other people had been driving the car on weekdays but when I offered $225 for the car, the owner accepted and just like that, I became a car owner.

As I only had $50 to make a down payment, I had to borrow the remaining $175. I was sure a bank wouldn't find me credit worthy so I went to M & J Finance Company. Their slogan was they would make loans to anybody. My payments were only $25 monthly for twelve months. I didn't stop to calculate the interest rate on that payment arrangement. It was something I thought I could handle.

Chapter 41
Hurricane Hazel

On Friday morning, October 15, 1954, the rain was coming down hard as I drove to work. The wind was blowing stronger than I anticipated. The weather forecast on Thursday evening had been all about a hurricane named Hazel. It was a large hurricane but predictions were it would probably bypass southeastern North Carolina.

Having lived inland all my life, I had never experienced the force of a hurricane. That was probably true of most coastal residents. Hurricanes and strong tropical storms mostly went ashore in Florida or even up in the New England area but seldom ever in the Wilmington area.

We didn't turn on our radio or TV that morning and had no idea that Hazel was already causing widespread destruction along the coast in Brunswick County. As I drove downtown, I did notice there were fewer cars on Market Street than usual.

I always parked my car on Water Street, between Dock and Orange, where there were no parking meters. I really got soaked that morning as I walked the block or so to the Kress store.

The manager, Mr. Hughey, and a few of the clerks were there. We discussed the option of not opening that morning but it seemed no one really knew what was about to fall on us so Mr. Hughey opted to open for business.

There was very little business. Only the snack counter, managed by Miss Prince, had any customers. All they wanted was a cup of coffee and someone to share any hurricane news they had.

As it became mid-morning, it was apparent that our decision to remain open was not a good one. The rain was coming down so hard, you could barely see the Baily Theatre just across the street. The winds were blowing things up and down the street, anything that wasn't fastened down, and in some instances, things that had been fastened down.

Awnings were being ripped off, signs were falling, and electrical power lines were snapping off the utility poles.

It was about this time, one of the floor supervisors, Mrs. Hilburn, decided she wanted to go home. Her home was in the Winnabow area, some twelve miles southwest of Wilmington. Her husband had brought her to work that morning and had planned to pick her up around 5:30 p.m. when the store closed.

Being young and foolish and wanting to have a better idea of what was really going on, I volunteered to take her home. I asked her to wait in the store while I walked to Water Street and got my car. To my surprise, the street was covered in one or two feet of water. I didn't know if it was the result of rain or if the Cape Fear River had overflowed its banks. Hazel picked the worst possible time to strike, just at the time of high tide.

I was able to start my car, drive up to Dock Street, then north on Front Street to the store. Mrs. Hilburn climbed in and off we went. There was only one bridge across the river then, the one at the northern end of town. Just as we reached the bridge, the storm abated, the clouds parted and the sun almost broke through the clouds. We thought the storm was over. Unfortunately, it was only the eye of the storm passing over.

The drive to Winnabow was almost pleasant, except for some trees that had blown over into the highway along with other debris and trash of assorted kinds. As I let Mrs. Hilburn out at her home, Hazel returned in full force.

The ride back to Wilmington was a nightmare. My car was being blown around so badly I could barely keep from running into the water filled ditches on either side. The rain was coming down in sheets in a sideways direction. Most of the time, I couldn't see where the road was. I feared I would never make it back to Wilmington again.

It took me about one hour to drive the twelve miles back to Wilmington. I felt I should go back to the store and finish out the day. A few people were still there although there was no power. Mr. Hughey finally told everyone they may as well go home. It didn't appear business was going to pick up that afternoon.

I drove home and pulled into the driveway. Seventh Street was covered with broken tree limbs, trash cans, chairs, porch swings, TV antennas, etc. Of course, the power was off on our street just as it was throughout the city. Our TV antenna was still attached to our chimney. The baling wire worked better than the guy wires and metal fasteners that the city required.

The next day was Saturday and I decided to report for work. Power had been restored to the downtown area and S. H. Kress & Co., was open and ready for business. Most of the activity in downtown Wilmington involved cleaning up the streets, repairing awnings, canopies and signs, and replacing broken windows.

Compared to the utter destruction at Carolina Beach and the beach towns in Brunswick County, the damage in Wilmington was minimal. In those towns, the utilities were non-functional, the streets were impassable, and people who had left their homes to escape Hazel weren't allowed to return.

All local National Guard units were mobilized and sent to the various beach towns to maintain law and order. Vernon and Leonard, had recently joined the National Guard and their unit, Company I, was deployed to Carolina Beach where they stayed for almost two weeks.

Without Vernon working in the stockroom, my job load was doubled while he was on National Guard duty. However, due to the diminished business, there wasn't as much to do. He and Leonard had a lot of "war stories" to share with me when they were finally released from active duty.

All young men in those days had an eight year military obligation. Vernon and Leonard didn't want to be drafted into the army so they had joined the National Guard. They convinced me of the advantages in serving in the National Guard as opposed to being a foot soldier in the army. I listened to their arguments and became a National Guardsman around the middle of November, 1954.

Chapter 42
Window Displays at S. H. Kress

We had just begun decorating the store with a Halloween motif when Hurricane Hazel came to our door and played tricks on us. Decorating the store for major holidays was a big deal. As with all retail stores, our holiday displays were designed to make the customers feel they absolutely had to buy those items on display if their holiday was to amount to anything. Most of the time, we fell short in attaining our objective.

Halloween was a real challenge although five and dime stores had an advantage over department stores. Very few people would go to Belk's, or Efird's, or Alexander's to buy costumes, false faces or candy. Kress's chief competitor, with respect to Halloween, was F. W. Woolworth. It was just up Front Street adjacent to the post office where huge numbers of people passed by its windows every day.

McLelland's and H. L. Green apparently didn't have display planners with much imagination. Our manager, Mr. Hughey, and the ladies who clerked at the counters that sold Halloween stuff would have a meeting in early September to make their plans. Mr. Hughey would have been advised by the district manager if there were any new Halloween "can't miss" items. Generally, there were not.

Halloween costumes along with scary false faces would be placed on the appropriate counter. Brach's Candy Company was the main source for Halloween candy. Candy corn was always a big seller. Of course, witches, black cats, and devils had a major role in Halloween decorations. One of the display windows out on Front Street was always crammed full of Halloween stuff.

Mr. Hughey would send one of the stock boys once or twice a week to take a peek at Woolworth's windows to ensure they weren't getting ahead of us in their display.

Halloween was hardly over before we had to start thinking about Thanksgiving decorations. We didn't offer very many items created specifically for Thanksgiving but we did have to put some posters and signs up throughout the store to remind our customers Thanksgiving was near. Paper napkins, plates, and cups with a Thanksgiving motif were about all we sold.

Christmas was the big holiday for store decorating. We would begin putting Christmas decorations up right after Thanksgiving. We didn't want Woolworth to get ahead of us. Christmas merchandise started arriving at the store in early October. Almost every counter had Christmas displays of some kind even though the merchandise on some of them had nothing to do with Christmas.

Instead of having only one display window with decorations, we would use three of the Front Street windows to show off what we had. One of the windows was used to display a highly-decorated Christmas tree. Unfortunately, no one at the store seemed to have a flair for decorating a Christmas tree. We could never get the tree to stand up straight. The lights, the balls, and the tinsel looked as if someone had blindfolded himself and thrown them at the tree. The angel hair made the tree look like it was having a bad hair day.

Of course, no store in Wilmington could compete with the large window at Belk's. Their manager must have given their decorating crew an unlimited budget. Everybody in the area would go to Belk's, sooner or later, to stand and marvel at their window. In the window, there were moving things, trains, elves, Mrs. Santa, little children, reindeer, and of course, Santa himself. Such large numbers of people gathered at the window you had to push yourself through the crowd in order to get a good view.

The city always had a big Christmas parade right down Front Street a few nights before Christmas Eve. It was a wonderful sight to see the street decorations the city had put up along with the highly decorated floats and to hear the bands playing Christmas music as they marched along.

Downtown stores would remain open after the parade in hopes some of the parade spectators would wander in and spend a little money. That's what happened at Kress's; they wandered in and spent very little money.

After the Christmas decorations were taken down and the Christmas merchandise put away, it was almost time to begin decorating for Valentine's Day. Valentine's Day didn't get much respect. We had to put out some Valentines and a few posters reminding customers to buy their sweetheart a card, if they wanted to live and do well.

The major contributor to the selling of Valentines was the long-time tradition of school children giving all their classmates a valentine. Even some NHHS students participated in this ritual to some extent.

I began to notice the manager of Kinney's Shoe Store come in almost every day around lunch time with his wife to look at the valentine cards. He would pull one off the counter, read the inscription to his wife and put the card back. She would then do the same for him. They would repeat this ritual every day until Valentine's Day. They never bought a card.

Easter was next. Although Easter was a Christian holiday, it was rapidly becoming more a commercial holiday. Our store followed all other stores in that respect. Many people believed commercialization really began when Gene Autry's version of "*Here Comes Peter Cottontail*" began outselling "*Up From The Grave He Arose*" by the Blackwood Brothers Quartet.

When Mr. Hughey and the floor supervisors met to make plans for our Easter display, Mr. Hughey invited me to participate as I had made some creative suggestions with respect to Christmas decorations. Mr. Hughey began the discussion with his usual question: "Does anyone have a good idea for this year's window decoration?"

Mrs. Hewett, the supervisor of the department where hardware as well as parakeets, goldfish, and pet supplies were sold said "My friend that works at Woolworth told me they were going to put five white rabbits in one of their windows and outside they'll have a speaker that'll play "Here Comes Peter Cottontail" about every five or ten minutes. And, of course, there'll be some Easter baskets with green grass and brightly colored Easter eggs."

Mr. Hughey was taken aback by this bit of news. "That's really creative," he said. "We've got to do better than that or we won't have anybody looking at us. Anybody got an idea?"

Nobody said anything so I thought I would make a suggestion. "How about if we put some canaries and parakeets in our window? We can keep bird food and water in there all the time and they can fly around in the window. People love to watch and listen to these pretty birds. You know, white rabbits are pretty but they don't do much, just lie around and sleep. Once you've seen a white rabbit lay around and sleep, you've pretty much seen enough of them. These canaries and parakeets are always active, flying around, hopping around, chirping, and fighting each other."

"Well," Mr. Hughey said. "That sounds good but what does it have to do with Easter?"

I thought for a minute. "You know, birds are a sign of spring. Easter comes in the spring. We can put some Easter lilies on the floor of the window and maybe hang some ladies Easter Bonnets from the ceiling. The bonnets will give the birds a place to perch."

"That's a pretty weak connection to Easter but I like the idea so let's go with it. I'll put you in charge, Kenan," Mr. Hughey told me

Easter was on Sunday, April 10, in 1955. I had plenty of time to make detailed plans. Mrs. Hewett and I worked together to make sure we had plenty of canaries and parakeets for the window display. Four or five of the ladies brought their old Easter bonnets from years gone by. I went down to Roudabush's and bought three big Easter lilies.

On the Sunday before Easter, I went down to the store by myself and put ten canaries, twenty-five parakeets, the Easter lilies and bonnets, and bowls for bird food and water in the window. I also put in a fake tree for perching purposes. The birds seemed to be greatly excited by having so much room to fly around as opposed to being cooped up in a bird cage.

I had to be very careful when putting the birds in the window as there was an opportunity for the birds already in the window to escape into the store when I opened the door to the window to put another bird or two in.

People across Front Street waiting to get into the Baily Theatre noticed what I was doing and several of them walked over to get a closer look. I hoped none of my former classmates at NHHS saw me playing around with canaries and parakeets.

The next day, Monday, the bird display was a big hit with passersby. Everyone had to stop and look at the birds for a few minutes. I walked up the street to Woolworth's and saw very few people stopped to look at white rabbits laying around sleeping even with *"Here Comes Peter Cottontail"* playing in the background.

We all felt pleased with our display. I did experience a bit of difficulty that afternoon in replenishing the food and water in the bowls. I hadn't thought that such little birds, even though there were twenty-five of them, could create such a mess with their droppings.

By the middle of Tuesday afternoon, Mr. Hughey told me I would have to go inside the window and do some cleaning. The floor, the window, and the Easter bonnets, were covered with bird droppings. I put on some rubber gloves, an old shirt and a baseball cap and went in with a bucket of water and a sponge.

While moving around in the window, some passersby stopped to look and offer advice as to where my cleaning would be most effective. I really hoped none of my former classmates came by.

As I bent over to clean up a spot on the floor near the front of the window, I accidentally knocked open the window door. I didn't realize what I had done until I suddenly noticed there were only a few birds in the window. Most of them had seized the opportunity to escape out into the store.

It took about two weeks to capture the birds that were flying all over the store, day and night. The store had a really high ceiling and we couldn't capture the birds until they came down looking for food and water.

Mr. Hughey asked me to remove the rest of the birds along with the display accessories and give the window a good scrubbing. We decided to replace the bird display with beach toys. As I walked by Woolworth's after work, I saw the white rabbits were still just lying around but overall the window and floor were pretty clean. However, there were several small bunny rabbits that hadn't been there before.

I was able to make up for this mistake in display judgement later that summer. Mr. Hughey' s wife was Greek and an ardent supporter of Greek holidays, especially Greek Independence Day which fell on March 25 each year. In 1829, Greece had finally won its independence from the Ottoman Empire and their Independence Day was as important to them as ours was to us.

Mrs. Hughey had persuaded Mr. Hughey to order huge quantities of sets of crockery with a Greek motif to be available for sale by Greek Independence Day. She believed people of Greek descent living in Wilmington, would snap up such beautifully decorated dinnerware, and there were lots of people in Wilmington of Greek descent. Many of the restaurants were owned by Greeks.

The crockery, dinner plates, soup bowls, salad bowls, cups and saucers, was decorated with an image of Iris, the Greek Goddess of the Rainbow. Iris was a very attractive goddess and the crockery wasn't too bad.

However, the people in Wilmington of Greek descent apparently didn't care too much for crockery with an image of Iris. We kept the crockery for a few months but really needed to get it out of our inventory. I suggested to Mr. Hughey that we put a display in one of the Front Street windows with a twenty-five percent off sign. He wanted to get this error in judgment behind him so he agreed.

I created a beautiful display of crockery and silverware. That afternoon, I saw Mr. Mike Zezefellis, owner of the Crystal Restaurant, just across the street, looking into the window. A few minutes later, both he and his brother, Mr. Theodore Zezefellis were looking.

The Zezefellis Brothers not only owned the Crystal Restaurant, they also were owners of the Crystal Fishing Pier at Wrightsville Beach. They came in and bought forty-five sets of crockery decorated with the image of the Greek Goddess Iris for their restaurant. They also bought forty-five sets of cutlery. It was one of the largest single purchases made at Kress's while I worked there.

1954 Top Songs, Movies and Books

Top Ten Songs
Little Things Mean A Lot by Kitty Kallen
Wanted by Perry Como
Hey There by Rosemary Clooney
Sh-Boom by The Crew Cuts
Make Love To Me by Jo Stafford
Oh! My Pa-pa by Eddie Fisher
I Get So Lonely by Four Knights
Three Coins in the Fountain by Four Aces
Secret Love by Doris Day
Hernando's Hideaway by Archie Bleyer

Top Five Movies
White Christmas with Bing Crosby, Danny Kaye, Rosemary
  Clooney, and Vera Ellen
20,000 Leagues Under The Sea with Kirk Douglas, James
  Mason and Peter Lorre
Rear Window with James Stewart and Grace Kelly
Demetrius and the Gladiators with Victor Mature, Anne
  Bancroft and Ernest Borgnine
The Caine Mutiny with Humphrey Bogart, Fred MacMurray
  and Van Johnson

Top Five Books
Not As a Stranger by Morton Thompson
Mary Anne by Daphne du Maurier

Love Is Eternal by Irving Stone
The Royal Box by Frances Parkinson Keyes
No Time For Sergeants by Mac Hyman

Chapter 43
Mr. Kenan Goes to Washington

My friend and co-worker, Vernon, decided he wasn't cut out to be a manager of a Kress five and dime store so in March, 1955, he resigned and went to work for Merritt-Holland Company. Among other things, Merritt-Holland sold welding supplies, including tanks of acetylene welding gas. By this time Vernon was an experienced truck driver, having driven his father's scrap metal truck, not only to NHHS but around the countryside picking up scrap metal with his father and brother. His job at Merritt-Holland was delivering the full cylinders of gas in the company truck to their customers and picking up the empty cylinders.

Not long after Vernon left S. H. Kress, I used my tremendous influence with Mr. Hughey to hire Leonard Williams to help in the stock room. Leonard was getting disillusioned at working in grocery stores, most notably the A & P. After I pointed out to him the wonderful opportunity to become a store manager at Kress, he decided he would follow in my footsteps.

At this time, Vernon was the owner of a 1952 Hudson Hornet, a very nice car, a car that was ideal for taking a long drive. I had been working steadily at Kress's for eleven months in July, 1955, and felt I needed a small vacation. Vernon, Leonard and I decided to take a sight-seeing trip to Washington, D.C. one weekend. Neither of us had been able to go on school trips to the nation's capitol. We planned to drive up on Friday, spend a couple of days and nights, and come back on Sunday.

We left early on Friday morning, stopped to eat lunch a little north of Richmond, and by five p.m., were in the outskirts of Washington. We were getting hungry and when we spotted what appeared to be a rustic-looking restaurant pulled off the highway and into the parking lot.

As we walked into the dimly lit restaurant, we noticed several men sitting at a bar. I assumed they were having a hot dog or hamburger for supper. The man behind the bar held up three fingers as we walked towards a table. Believing he was asking if we wanted a table with three chairs, I nodded "Yes,"

The jukebox was playing "Ain't That a Shame" by Fats Domino. Behind the bar, on a shelf, the CBS evening news program, "Douglas Edwards with the News," was airing. Mr. Edwards was interviewing Senator Estes Kefauver from Tennessee. He had announced he was seeking to be the Democratic candidate for president in 1956. He had on his traditional coonskin cap which seemed appropriate for a senator from Tennessee.

His main opponent, he said, would be Adlai Stevenson who had lost so badly to President Eisenhower in 1952, 442 electoral votes to 89. Senator Kefauver was known for his liberal policies and he was really letting President Eisenhower, a Republican, have it with both barrels of his political gun.

Two men sitting at the bar, who were intently watching the TV news, suddenly began arguing. Apparently, one was a democrat and the other a republican.

The republican supporter was not hesitant in letting his opponent know his opinions of Senator Kefauver. "Look at that fool," he said. "He ain't got the sense of a coon. If he ever gets to be president, his major policy will probably be to make everybody wear a coonskin cap. He'll want the federal government to take over everything, maybe give everybody a coonskin cap. He's probably owns a coonskin cap factory."

The other gentleman expressed his views; "Look where we are now under Eisenhower and Nixon. The poor get poorer and the rich get richer. And that Nixon, he'd make a good used car salesman. There's no telling what he's up to."

Almost immediately, the air was filled with profanities and obscenities that we had never heard in Wilmington. The two men began shoving each other. The bartender, an unusually large and mean looking man, came between them and told them to take it outside if they were going to fight. They rushed to the door and disappeared.

The bartender walked over to our table with three huge glasses of draft beer and set them down. "That'll be three dollars, gents," he said. "What?" I exclaimed. "We didn't order any beer."

"You sure did. When you came in, I asked if you wanted three glasses and you're the very one who nodded yes. Are you gonna pay or not?" He asked as he leaned over and put his big hands on the table.

We looked at each other. Neither of us drank but considering the size and the bartender's mean look, we each pulled out a dollar and handed it to him. He walked back to the bar.

Since we had bought a beer, I decided to give it a try. That was the worst tasting stuff I had ever had in my mouth. Vernon and Leonard looked at my expression and decided not to indulge. We put our glasses down and walked quickly out the restaurant.

As we passed the bartender, he asked "You boys through already?" "Yes sir," I said. "We just remembered we're late for a meeting and have to run."

When we got outside, the two men were still yelling profanities and obscenities and shoving each other around but no blows were being thrown. Being a staunch republican, I was hoping the republican gentleman would prevail but we had to move on before the argument was settled.

We drove on towards Washington and soon saw a billboard that was advertising White Castle Hamburgers for ten cents each. Hamburgers sounded real good and the price sounded even better so we stopped at the store. It was pretty busy but we were able to get a table. When our hamburgers were ready, we couldn't believe the size. They were only one-fourth the size of hamburgers at the Miljo or the Chic-Chic in Wilmington. They were very good, but so small, Leonard ate six of them without any trouble.

We wanted to stay as near as possible to the Smithsonian Museum, the White House, the Washington Monument and the Capitol Building. We eventually ended up at the Mayflower Hotel although the room rate was really high: $4.50 per night for three people. For the two nights we stayed there, we had to pay $9.00 plus tax.

The advantage in staying at the Mayflower was we could walk to most of the places we wanted to see. The weather was perfect, the people were friendly, and the Smithsonian Museum was incredible. The museum in Wilmington didn't have half as much stuff as the Smithsonian.

On Saturday night, we were in our hotel room and decided we to walk down the street and see a movie. Not used to staying in a motel, we saw an Exit sign over a door and opened the door to walk out. Immediately, a loud alarm went off. It scared the pants off us. We ran back down the hallway, jumped into our room and slammed the door. We were sure we would probably be arrested for some serious hotel infraction. Nothing happened.

After a long wait, I opened the door, looked up and down the hallway and saw no hotel detectives or other law enforcement officials. We emerged from our room, walked through the lobby this time and went to see the movie: "*Bad Day at Black Rock.*" Even with only one arm Spencer Tracy could outwit and out fight the bad guys.

We arose early Sunday morning and headed back to Wilmington. We didn't try to go through the exit door but went through the lobby and paid our hotel bill like normal people. I wanted to leave a quarter as a tip for the maid; something I had learned from Mr. Hobbs, our District Manager, but Vernon and Leonard overruled me.

Chapter 44
Our Seventh Move in Five Years

When I got back home on Sunday evening, Mother told me she had decided to move again. She had seen an ad in Friday's morning paper a six room house at 26 Central Boulevard was available for only $50 a month. A six room house with a bath would definitely be a better fit for our family than an apartment on Seventh Street. She called the owner and agreed to rent the home

She told me she had tried to get Williams Moving Company to do the moving on Saturday but they were busy and couldn't do it. "Do you mean to tell me you were going to move while I was gone? That sounds like something we've been through before," I said.

"Well, I didn't think of that. Gerald and Coleman were out of school on Saturday and they could have helped. And besides, I can tell Mrs. Henly is ready for us to move. Coleman and his rowdy friends are about to drive her crazy. And Coleman's little dog is always pulling her wash off the clothes line. I have to pacify her every wash day," she said.

As Williams Moving Company had a moving job on Tuesday, Mr. Williams told Mother she should call the Rabunsky Transfer Company. He knew Mr. Rabunsky personally and highly recommended him. Mr. Rabunsky worked out of his home in Lake Village.

I was able to persuade Mr. Hughey to let me off work on Tuesday so I could help with the move. As we were loading our household goods into Mr. Rabunsky's truck, Mrs. Henly came out of her apartment and asked me, with a hopeful look on her face, if we were moving. I told her we hated to move away from her but we had lived there longer than we normally did and it was time to move again.

The house at 26 Central Boulevard was nice but somewhat noisy. It was close to the State Ports and train whistles, ship horns, and large trucks on Burnett Boulevard could be heard day and night. The front yard was rather small but there was room to play badminton which we often did over the next few months. The back yard was a mess; a couple of old fallen-in storage sheds, lots of weeds, and some old discarded furniture.

26 Central Boulevard

Our next door neighbor was Mrs. Selena Lewis. She lived there with her son, George, who was a year older than me. Mrs. Selena was the collections agent for Hufham's Credit Clothiers, a men's clothing store on South Front Street in Wilmington. Collecting required her to ride all over New Hanover County tracking down the late payers or the no-payers. According to her, Mr. Huffham wasn't very careful in verifying the credit worthiness of his customers. She was okay with that as his sloppy credit checking resulting in her having a full time job.

I didn't know it at the time, but Mrs. Selena was related to the family of my future wife, Millie Maultsby. She and some of her family occasionally visited Mrs. Selena while I was living at 26 Central Boulevard. She may have been playing in the yard next door while I was playing in our yard and we didn't know what the future held in store for us.

South Front Street, between Market and Dock, was a hotbed for men's clothing stores: in addition to Huffham's there were Leeds' Men's Shop, D'Lugin's, Checkner's, and Nathan's Clothiers. D'Lugin's was reputed to have a clerk stand outside the store and, with a hook on a pole, pull men and boys into their store.

There were some advantages to living on Central Boulevard. We lived very close to the National Guard Armory, to Legion Stadium and to my favorite barber shop, Teague's Barber Shop, just up the street on the corner of Carolina Beach Road and Central Boulevard.

A disadvantage to living on Central Boulevard was I had to take Coleman to Tileston every school morning and Gerald to New Hanover on most school mornings. Also, a lady who was known only as Miss Prince, the manager of the lunch counter at Kress's, depended on me to give her a ride to work every day. We were generally a very grouchy group on most mornings. On Friday mornings, the last day of the school week, Gerald and Coleman were happy, but not so Mrs. Prince, who never seemed to be happy.

My old '49 Ford was resisting the increased mileage I was now driving. When we lived on Seventh Street, Gerald and Coleman walked to school, Mrs. Prince rode the city bus to

Kress's, and it was only a half mile from our home to downtown Wilmington.

Sometimes I had to get Gerald and Coleman to help push the car to get it started. The three of us, put together, weren't very strong but usually we could get the car going fast enough so I could jump in and with skilled manipulation of the clutch and accelerator get the motor running.

One morning Mr. Hughey asked to borrow my car to drive to Goldsboro for a merchandise meeting. He had been in an accident and his car wasn't drivable. I had some reservations about such a long out-of-town trip for the car but was afraid to say no.

He told me when he returned late that afternoon the car wouldn't start when the meeting was over and he had to get several of the Kress store managers to give him a push. He felt his dignity had been compromised by such an unfortunate incident. He never asked to borrow my car again.

One evening as I was driving home on Burnett Boulevard, a policeman pulled me over. He walked up to my window and asked to see my driver's license. He then walked around the car and stopped at the left front fender.

"What happened to your fender?" He asked. "It looks like you've hit something recently."

"Yessir," I answered. "I was pulling into my driveway yesterday evening and accidentally bumped into our mailbox post. It made a big dent, didn't it?"

"I just got word on my radio that a car like this'un was involved in a hit and run accident at the intersection of Third and Greenfield. A truck with a lot of chickens was run into and dozens of chickens are running all over everywhere. Did you come that way?"

"No sir," I replied. "I came down Front Street. I work at Kress's dime store and I don't ever come home on Third Street."

Just then we heard a voice on his radio saying the hit and run driver had been caught. He had been spotted driving around Greenfield Lake and had run off the road into a tree while being chased by the police.

"Okay, you can go, young man," the policeman said. "But I'm not sure I believe your story about running into a mailbox post. That dent looks worse than a mailbox post would cause."

Actually, he was right. A few nights earlier while driving down Market Street, I decided to make a left turn at Fifth and Market. As everyone knows there is a huge water fountain, the Kenan Memorial Fountain, sitting in the middle of that intersection and left turns are not allowed. I was in a hurry, it was dark, and I saw no one coming so I decided to break the law and made a left turn onto Fifth Street. Another car suddenly came out of nowhere, speeding, no doubt, and I bumped into the fountain to avoid a wreck. Since the fountain wasn't damaged very much, I decided to get away from there as fast as I could.

Repairing or replacing the starter, or removing dents, didn't fit into my budget. Neither did keeping the tires in good condition. One Saturday night while out on a date, I had two flat tires. Luckily, I had a badly worn spare tire to take care of the first flat and was able to get my date back home. The second flat happened when I was only two or three blocks from home and walked the rest of the way. Vernon helped me fix the flat the next day, Sunday.

The radiator leaked badly. In order to prevent the car from overheating, I kept a large container of water in the trunk at all times so I could refill the radiator as needed, which was quite often.

Due to some faulty thinking, when our National Guard unit went to Ft. Bragg for a weekend of training, I decided to drive my old Ford rather than riding in a National Guard truck in which most of the Guardsmen rode. Vernon and Leonard rode with me. About halfway between Elizabethtown and Ft. Bragg, the car gave up. It refused to go any further.

Luckily, we were ahead of the National Guard trucks. We were standing there looking at the car when they came by. They stopped and we threw our gear into one of the trucks and went on to Ft. Bragg. As we rode off, I looked back at my old car and, sad to say, had some derogatory thoughts.

All the next day, during our vigorous military training, I kept thinking about how I was going to get my car. That Saturday we were practicing our marksmanship with the M-1 rifle. On the firing range, half our unit would be on the firing line while the other half would be in the pits, marking the target where the bullets hit.

The firing line was 100 yards from the targets. Each target was mounted on a board about five feet wide and five feet high. After each shooter had fired his rounds, the men in the pits would pull the target down and place black markers where the bullets hit and then pull the target back up so the officers who were doing the grading could see how well, or how poorly, the shooter was doing.

I was on the firing line early and qualified as a sharpshooter. That afternoon I was in the pits along with Vernon, Leonard, and several others. Our men on the firing line that afternoon weren't doing very good with their marksmanship so we decided to help them by placing the markers in various places but always fairly close to the bullseye. Our company was recognized for scoring well above average.

Leonard   Kenan   Vernon

After learning of my car problem, Lieutenant Keen, who had driven his car to Ft. Bragg, volunteered to go back with me that evening after our exercises were over for the day. Lt. Keen was the manager of the Ford service department in civilian life. It didn't take him long to diagnose the problem as a faulty coil. We rode back to Fayetteville, purchased a coil from the Ford dealer, and before it got dark, we had my car running again and parked behind our barracks.

Rather than putting money into an old car, I decided to look around for a better, newer car. While walking around downtown on my lunch hour looking at the used cars, I spotted one that caught my attention: a 1949 Dodge Coronet on the Baugh Motor Co. car lot at Second and Grace Streets.

It was a black classy looking car, the kind a company executive would drive. As I was on my way up the corporate ladder, a manager trainee with S. H. Kress & Co., I thought I would look good in that car.

One feature I really liked was something called fluid drive. I didn't understand how it worked but its advantage was the driver could come to a stop in any gear without using the clutch, even on a hill, and then go on without shifting gears or using the clutch. I desperately needed a feature like that as I was constantly losing control of my car when I had to stop on a hill. I would either roll back down the hill or the engine would shut off.

The price, $195, after a trade-in, was more than I wanted to pay but I would look so good in that car and it would be so easy to drive without shifting gears. I felt I had to have it. After visiting M & J Finance Co., who agreed to loan me the money, I left my old Ford with Mr. Baugh and drove off in my bright and shiny 1949 Dodge Coronet.

In order to test the fluid drive feature of my Dodge Coronet, I drove over to the driver's licensing office and drove through the course that applicants had to drive. My Dodge performed without a hitch, even at the top of the hill where I had so much trouble when I was trying to get my driver's license.

Chapter 45
Moving Up the Corporate Ladder

After having worked at Kress's for seven months in the manager trainee program, more responsibilities were given to me. I was spending more time on the sales floor rather than filling orders for the sales counters, arranging displays, taking money from the cash registers at the end of the day, putting a certain amount of money into the cash registers each morning, calculating the payroll each Monday and putting the correct amount of pay into envelopes to hand out to the employees, ordering items to replenish our inventory, and a limited amount of hiring and firing employees.

Just the thought of terminating an employee made my stomach hurt. Fortunately, I wasn't called on to do that very often. The one employee I had continuing trouble with was out janitor, Preston. He was often late for work or didn't come in at all, and sometimes came in half-drunk. I threatened to fire him several times if he didn't straighten up.

The final straw came on the day he refused to sweep the floor. I had no choice but to let him go. He came back in three days later, pleading for another chance. As soft-hearted as I was, I agreed and let him return. That afternoon, he asked me to lend him $12 to pay a speeding ticket. I barely had $12 but I loaned him the money. A few days later, he came to work half-drunk and I fired him again. I never did get my $12 back.

Our office manager was beginning to hear rumors from our corporate office in New York I was going to be transferred to another store. On March 10, 1956, I was supposed to be transferred shortly to the New Bern store. On April 20, I was supposed to be transferred to Roanoke, Virginia. On April 30, 1956, I learned I was definitely going to be transferred to the Raleigh store.

Meanwhile, Mr. Hughey, the store manager, learned he was to be transferred to the New Bern store almost immediately. The new store manager for our store, Mr. Brooks, couldn't arrive for a week and I was left in charge of the store until he arrived.

I felt pretty important, only nineteen years old, to be in charge of such a large store with so many employees. Mr. Hughey had told Mr. Hobbs, our District Manager, what a good job I was doing for the store. I was fortunate he didn't mention to Mr. Hobbs the canary and parakeet window display fiasco.

My sense of importance was somewhat diminished on Saturday morning, April 7, 1956. I wanted to get a good view of the Azalea Festival Parade as it came down Front Street. One of my favorite actresses, Polly Bergen, the Pepsi-Cola girl, was the Azalea Queen and she was riding on the last float in the parade. Among other movies, she had starred in three of the Dean Martin-Jerry Lewis movies.

About the time for the last float to come by, I went up to the second floor of our store and tried to open a window. The window had frosted glass so I had to open it in order to see the parade. It was stuck and in my efforts to get it open, it broke and my hand was cut pretty badly. The broken glass fell on the canopy below so it didn't hurt anyone.

Miss Bergen heard the noise and looked up to the window. She saw me standing there with my hand up in the air to stop the bleeding and thought I was waving to her. She kissed her hand and waved at me. I was thrilled to think that the Pepsi-Cola girl had noticed me but meanwhile my hand was bleeding profusely and I needed to get to a doctor.

I found Leonard on Front Street in front of Kress's and asked him to walk up the street with me to Bullock Hospital, just up the street at 221 North Front. When we walked in, the receptionist saw my trouble and called to a doctor who happened to pass by. The doctor, Doctor William Mebane, took me into an office and with a couple of stitches soon stopped the bleeding.

As we talked, I realized Dr. Mebane was the father of one of my classmates, Roxanna Mebane. After learning Roxanna was a classmate, Dr. Mebane became very friendly and wanted to know more about what I had been doing after graduating from NHHS.

He told me he and two other doctors, Drs. Robey Sinclair and Samuel Pace, had recently purchased from the county a tract of land on Wrightsville Avenue on which Wessell Tuberculosis Sanitarium had been located. They planned to construct a small hospital on the tract of land in 1957. They believed James Walker Memorial Hospital and Bullock

Hospital could not handle all the hospital traffic in New Hanover County. [13]

When I got back to Kress's, everyone wanted to see my hand with the stitches. I assured everyone I was okay but begged them not to tell Mr. Hobbs or the new store manager, scheduled to arrive shortly, about my accident. I didn't think it would look good on my resume.

Chapter 46
Assistant Store Manager

On Sunday, May 13, 1956, after saying goodbye to my family and asking Mother not to move while I was away without telling me, I left for Raleigh. On my last day in Wilmington, I went to Efird's Department Store and bought some new clothes, including a gray suit. I was unable to get a date that night so I went to the Bailey Theatre by myself and saw Gregory Peck and Jennifer Jones in the movie *"The Man in the Gray Flannel Suit"*. I wondered if that was a good or a bad omen.

The clerk in the men's clothing department at Efird's talked me into buying a double-breasted suit. It wasn't that hard to do. I had recently seen a movie with Mickey Rooney and Judy Garland in which Mickey wore a double-breasted suit. As Mickey was short like me and as he looked very mature in that suit, I thought a suit like he wore would do the same for me. Mother didn't like my new suit when I showed it to her that night. Gerald and Coleman told me I looked like Leo Gorcey.[14]

I felt very mature driving my Cornet Dodge with fluid drive to Raleigh on my way to be an assistant manager at a

---

[13] Cape Fear Hospital opened in August, 1957. On opening day patients paid $3 for an office visit, $10 for a physical, and, if hospitalized, $8 a day for a private room.

[14] Leo Gorcey was the leader of a gang, the Bowery Boys, who starred in several grade B movies in the 1950's, generally shown at the Bijou but never at the Bailey. The Bowery Boys were always in trouble but it was never their fault.

five and dime store. I would be paid $60 weekly in that position. I felt rich, so rich I decided to spend Sunday night at the luxurious Sir Walter Raleigh Hotel in downtown Raleigh even though it cost me three dollars.

I arose early on Monday morning, checked out of the Sir Walter Raleigh, ate breakfast at the S & W Cafeteria, and walked into S. H. Kress at 7:45 AM. Mr. Schultz, the manager, and Mr. Miller, an assistant manager, were there to meet me.

I wanted to make good first impression so I wore my new suit. I was shocked when I saw Mr. Schultz was wearing a double-breasted suit just like mine. What was really strange was we both had the same tie. Mr. Schultz was about six feet, four inches tall and I was only five feet, six inches tall. As we walked around the Kress store being introduced to all the sales ladies, we must have been a strange looking pair. I never wore the suit to work again.

As I didn't have the foresight to get to Raleigh earlier and find a place to stay, Mr. Schultz looked through the newspaper at the rental ads and advised me which places would be better for me.

I decided to look first at a room at 917 W. Johnson Street. It turned out to be a very nice room with a separate bath and entrance; $20 a month in the basement of a home owned by a Mr. and Mrs. Coats. It was only one and one-half miles to downtown Raleigh where S. H. Kress was located. The store was across the street from the State Capitol Building. It had one entrance on Salisbury Street and another on Fayetteville Street. It was much larger than the store in Wilmington.

I was assigned, as an assistant manager, to the basement sales floor. Hardware, crockery, pet supplies, plants and flowers, toys, some furniture, and a large lunch counter were located in the basement. I didn't know what I was doing or supposed to do half the time. I just walked around with a confident look on my face.

On my third day in Raleigh, I lost much of my confidence. While changing a display, I broke a piece of glass and then broke the door for the display. I left my bedroom window up that morning and it rained heavily all day. That night I had to give a class on the .30 caliber machine gun at the National

Guard meeting and that was a flop. It took several days to get that confident look back on my face.

S. H. Kress Asst. Manager – 1956
(Not my car)

On June 30, 1956, I received a letter from Mother telling me they had moved again, this time to 609 South Fifth Street, the eighth move in six years. I appreciated the fact she informed me of the move so I knew where to go the next time I went home.

Although I generally couldn't get out of Raleigh on Saturday evenings until six or seven o'clock, I went home almost every weekend. Some weekends, I didn't leave Raleigh until early Sunday morning. Of course, I had to be at work early Monday mornings so I always returned to Raleigh on Sunday evenings.

On my way home late one Saturday, I picked up a hitchhiker near Clinton. It turned out to be Stewart Hare, a classmate at NHHS. Many NHHS graduates were attending college in Raleigh: North Carolina State College, Peace College, St. Mary's College and Meredith. Some of them occasionally did some shopping at Kress's.

If they came into the basement and saw me hard at work breaking display windows, etc., they would stop and talk awhile. Ed Dye, Joe Tardugno, and Ed Caldwell, among others, came by. One day Patsy Barrett came through. She and I had been in several classes together including French II under Mr. T. G. Browning. She had also written daily articles for the Wilmington Star-News that gave all the interesting details about the parties, dances, student elections, student plays, student trips, etc., that occurred at NHHS. She had done this for three years.

On this occasion, she informed me she was engaged to Lee Terrill, the coach of the freshman basketball team at N. C. State University. I was so impressed. N. C. State was my favorite basketball team. I was excited to think I knew someone who knew someone who played for Everett Case's team. I remember reading Lee was drafted by the Fort Wayne Pistons in the 1952 NBA draft.

I was surprised and pleased to see two of my old friends from Chinquapin, Molly James and Conrad Sloan, stop by one day. Although I hadn't seen either of them in almost six years, we still had some good memories from Chinquapin School to share.

One weekend in November, I was assigned to work at the Kress store in Wilmington as the manager had to be out of town for a few days. I enjoyed my brief managerial stint there. Leonard was still working there as were most of the same salesladies.

On Friday afternoon, I got a phone call from Mother to tell me Coleman had suffered a broken leg while playing football for Tileston. He had been taken to James Walker Hospital and she wanted me to rush over there and be with him. It was closing time when she called so I asked Leonard to go with me.

When we arrived, we found Coleman was almost ready to go home. In order to set his broken leg, the pants of his football uniform had to be cut off and removed. He would need some clothing to wear home when released from the hospital. I asked Leonard to take a taxi to our home to get some pants for Coleman to wear home while I stayed with him.

He was kind enough to do that for me. However, when he arrived at our home, things didn't go as well for him as they should have for someone who was on a mission of mercy. He asked the taxi driver to wait for him while he went in to get Coleman's pants.

Mother and Joan happened to be home at the time. When Leonard explained to them he needed some pants for Coleman to wear home, they thought Coleman was waiting out in the taxi, and it was their opinion if Coleman had managed to get out of the hospital, into the taxi, and all the way across town to our house without any pants, he could darn well get from the taxi into the house without any.

There was some lack of communication apparently; Leonard couldn't make them understand Coleman was still back at the hospital waiting for his pants. They were determined not to let Leonard carry any pants to Coleman for such a short distance. Perhaps they thought Leonard was using this as a clever ruse to get a pair of pants for himself.

After a difficult and confusing exchange of questions, answers and accusations, they finally understood what the situation was and reluctantly gave him Coleman's best pants so he would look his best upon leaving the hospital.

Chapter 47
Social Life of a Manager Trainee

I would have enjoyed my weekend trips to Wilmington more if my Dodge Coronet with fluid drive wasn't constantly giving me trouble. I couldn't be sure that I would make it to Wilmington or back to Raleigh. Generators for Dodge Coronets must have been made in Japan. I had to replace the generator twice in a month. Perhaps I should have bought a new generator rather than one from a junk yard but the junk yard generators were so much cheaper.

Due to faulty generators, the battery was never fully charged. I had to be pushed numerous times in order to get the car cranked. Pushing a large Dodge Cornet with fluid drive had to be done by another vehicle. Pushing it by man power couldn't get the car going fast enough for the engine to catch.

Sometimes when the car wouldn't start, I would be in a place where getting someone to push me was next to impossible. One Saturday night while in Wilmington, my date and I went to see *War and Peace* at the Baily Theatre. We decided to sit on the back row in the balcony. During all my days as an usher at the Bailey, I had never sat in that hallowed place. Some of the same couples on the back row were the same ones I once watched while working in the balcony for blacks back in 1953.

The movie was unusually long, three and one-half hours. It took a long time for the Russians to run Napoleon and his gang back to France. Also, there was, in my opinion, some bad miscasting; Audrey Hepburn as Natasha and Henry Fonda as Pierre just weren't able to play believable characters. Natasha was supposed to be spontaneous, charming, and vivacious and Audrey couldn't quite carry that off. Pierre was supposed to be a large, somewhat bulky, man. Henry Fonda wasn't even close.

It was late when we left the Baily only to discover that my car wouldn't start. My solution was to put her on the city bus for a ride to her home while I rode a different bus to my home on Central Boulevard. She indicated she would prefer a taxi but I was running short of funds. I had already exceeded my date budget:

I had taken her out to eat at Futrelle's Pharmacy where we had a chicken salad sandwich and a Pepsi-Cola. The movie ticket was fifty-five cents each and she had to have a big bag of popcorn and another Pepsi. As the bus went within two blocks of her home, I thought the bus ride was satisfactory. She was always busy when I asked her for another date afterwards.

The winter of 1956/57 was very cold and my car derived pleasure in not starting on particularly cold mornings. It seemed to snow or sleet once or twice a week. Some mornings, the temperature would be in the teens. After trying for several minutes to start the car, I would give up and wait fifteen or twenty minutes for the city bus to come by for a ride to work.

On those mornings when it did crank, it was certain not to start in the evening after work. Mr. Schultz, the store manager, and Mr. Miller, the other assistant store manager, were very patient with me. If the car wouldn't start in the morning, one of them would carry me home after work and push my car to get it started. If the car wouldn't start in the evening, one of them would push me to get it started. In January, 1957, I required nine pushes during a period of thirteen days.

I always took my car to the same service station for service. It was owned by Mr. Norwood Dail, formerly of Chinquapin. I believed he would give me a good deal which he did but my car never seemed to get repaired. My motto was if you couldn't trust someone from Chinquapin, who could you trust?

Not only did my Dodge Cornet have mechanical troubles but it was a target for other drivers. There were several scrapes on both sides where hit and run drivers had driven by too closely. While at work on one Thursday, a hit and run driver sideswiped my car and did considerable damage. The other sideswipes were minor so I didn't even report them to the police.

However, this time, the damage was too severe to ignore. Somehow, the police were able to catch the driver the next day. His insurance company was forced to pay for the damage. When the insurance adjuster came by he declared my car had already been damaged before his client hit it. I eventually had to take the claim to Small Claims Court and it ruled in my favor. The repair bill was only $109. Based on the intensity of the fight the insurance company put up, you would have thought the cost was in the thousands of dollars.

I was almost afraid to ask a girl for a date for fear we wouldn't make it to where we wanted to go or make it back home. I really hated to put another date on the city bus. However, there was one girl, Joy Jones, who worked on the toy counter that sometimes would almost ask me to ask her for a date. Manager trainees weren't supposed to fraternize with employees so I didn't respond for a long time.

On one Thursday, Joy told me she was quitting on Saturday and again asked me to come see her. As she would no longer be an employee, we made a date for the following Thursday night. She gave me detailed instructions on how to get to her home which was off Highway 50 between Raleigh and Benson.

After getting lost several times, I finally drove up. Her entire family was sitting on the porch as if they wanted to interview me before allowing me to enter the house. I wouldn't have entered the house anyway if I could avoid it. It was even worse than some of the houses in Mill Swamp at Chinquapin.

She introduced me to her mother and daddy, both of which had bad breath as did her younger two sisters. They all looked as if they had put in a hard day's work at the tobacco barn. Her father's name was Jolly and her mother's name was Merry. Their dispositions didn't come close to what you might expect from two people with the names of Jolly and Merry.

She had two younger sisters with the names of Grace and Mercy. When I was introduced to them, the words of Psalm 23, verse 6, King James Version, popped into my head: *"Surely goodness and mercy shall follow me all the days of my life."* I guess Jolly and Merry Jones didn't have the nerve to name of their daughters, Goodness.

Mr. Jones wasn't bashful; he got right to the point. After a few minutes of enlightening conversation, he asked, "How much do you make at that dime store?"

I was surprised by his question and answered truthfully before I had time to think. "Well, right now, I'm getting sixty dollars a week."

"Did you hear that, Joy? Looks like you got a good one this time," he said. I instantly recognized I had made a big mistake in sharing my compensation figures.

He then asked where I intended to go with Joy. I had earlier thought of going to a movie but after meeting her family, I was trying to think of a shorter time period for our date. "Well, I don't have any definite plans; maybe just go for a short ride over to Benson to a drive-in restaurant. I haven't eaten supper yet, have you, Joy?"

"Hey, that's a good idee," Mr. Jones said. "We ain't had supper yet, either. It'd be a good time for us all to go together and get to know one another. How about that idee?"

I felt I couldn't refuse his gracious offer. I didn't have the nerve to tell him no. Joy and Mercy got in the front seat with me and Jolly, Merry, and Grace climbed into the back seat, and off we went to Benson. There was a drive-in restaurant on

East Main Street on the southern edge of town where I had eaten before on my weekend trips to and from Wilmington.

I never knew a family that ate so much; hot dogs, hamburgers, milkshakes and ice cream. My car looked like a trash dump after everybody ate their fill. When the curb girl presented her bill, Mr. Jones exclaimed, "Well, I'll be John Brown, I forgot to bring any money. Kenan, why don't you pay for everybody and I'll settle up with you when we get home?"

I barely had enough money to pay the bill. I took them home on the shortest route possible. I told them I needed to get back to Raleigh as I had noticed the headlights were getting dimmer and it was likely the generator wasn't working.

I waited to hear from Mr. Jones about settling up with me but he got out and walked into their house without saying a word about the bill.

Joy wanted to know when I could come back to see her. I told her as soon as I could afford a new generator for my car. As I sped off back to Raleigh, I thought I would never have them in my car again if I could help it. I didn't want Jolly, Merry, Joy, Grace and Mercy following me all the days of my life.

Although my Dodge had caused me a lot of trouble over the past few months, I think it may have saved my life on that particular occasion.

Other than my date with Joy, my social life was limited to playing on our National Guard basketball team. We played some of our games in the William Neal Reynolds Coliseum. It was exciting to play where so many outstanding players for the North Carolina State Wolfpack had played. Other games were played in a gym located on the grounds of the Dorthea Dix Hospital, a psychiatric hospital, more commonly known as Dix Hill.

It seemed strange to play in a gym that was surrounded by buildings in which hundreds of people lived that were mentally challenged. As players on the two teams pushed, shoved, and cursed each other, and the referee, an impartial observer may have thought some of the Dix Hill residents were out on the court playing basketball

Chapter 48
Out of the Frying Pan

In late November, 1956, I was becoming unhappy with the career path I had chosen, manager trainee at S. H. Kress & Co. Perhaps it wasn't my destiny to hire and fire people, to deal with numerous unhappy, uncooperative salesclerks and customers, to create imaginative displays, or to work sixty hours a week for $60.

I wondered if an honor graduate from New Hanover High School in Wilmington, North Carolina, shouldn't have been able to do better than work at a five and dime store.

We were informed on November 30 that Mr. S. H. Kress himself was coming to inspect our store on December 10. We began scampering around like madmen trying to get the store ready for a visit by the most important person in the world in our eyes. Rather than working only ten hours a day, we worked twelve hours. Mr. Schultz, the store manager, never seemed satisfied with the way things were shaping up. We were getting stressed out as the big day for the big guy's visit got closer.

On the big day, Mr. Kress arrived on schedule, stayed about five minutes and took off to look at the Kress store in Durham. We were all upset we had worked so hard and so long without getting hardly a "Hi, how are you?"

On January 7, 1957, Mr. Schultz told me I was to go to Hempstead, Long Island, New York, in February to help with a new store opening. I was fairly excited about this. It would give me an opportunity to do some serious sight-seeing in New York City.

However, my excitement died and turned to dread when, a week later, Mr. Schultz told me it was to be a permanent assignment. I could hardly believe the S. H. Kress Company needed somebody from Mill Swamp, North Carolina, to help manage a store on Long Island, New York.

I immediately began thinking of alternatives to accepting the assignment. I desperately wanted a skill that would enable me to make a decent living. The only jobs I ever had were cropping tobacco, picking beans and strawberries, ushering at a theatre, working as a soda jerk, a very short stint working in a grocery store, and serving one day as a student county commissioner in New Hanover County.

I began thinking of the military. I believed, according to the recruiting ads, that enlistees would have their choice of multiple vocations in service. My research led me to believe the Air Force would be my best choice. I read an airman could select a career field that would give him the education and training needed to start his own business or at least get a wonderful job working in that field for some large company. My dream was to learn how to repair radios and television sets. As television was becoming such a large industry and with millions of TV sets out there in TV land, a large percentage of them, sooner or later, would need repairs.

On January 21, during my lunch hour, I walked over to the Air Force recruiting office and had a long discussion with him. The next day, I took the screening test and passed. Actually, I think any idiot could have passed. The recruiter told me I did so well I was qualified to attend Officer Candidate School. He added when I arrived at Lackland Air Force Base in Texas to tell my DI I was a candidate for OCS.

On January 23, I went through a physical exam and almost passed out when a blood sample was taken. I think as long as the enlistee didn't die, he would have passed the physical. I hadn't gained much weight since finishing New Hanover High School in 1954. I weighed a hefty 120 pounds.

I worked my last day for Kress on Saturday, January 26, 1957. I drove my Dodge Coronet with fluid drive home that weekend and said goodbye to everyone. Leonard drove me back to Raleigh on Sunday evening and took my car back home.

The next day, I caught the bus to the recruiting office where dozens of other enlistees were hanging around. We were driven out to the Raleigh-Durham airport just after dark and put on a plane. It was my first airplane flight. We flew all night to San Antonio where Lackland AFB is located. I stared out the window all the way but wasn't able to see a thing from the air, something I had really looked forward to.

We landed just as daylight appeared and were rushed off the plane. An Air Force bus and a Drill Instructor were waiting for us. As he tried to get us into a military formation,

I heard the most outstanding obscene and profane words I had ever heard.

After the DI had gotten us organized, I raised my hand and told him the recruiter had told me I was a candidate for OCS.

"Yeah, ain't you all?" He said with a scornful smile. "All you idiots that were told by your recruiter that you were a candidate for OCS take one step forward."

Everyone stepped forward. We all stared at each other while the DI laughed out loud. "You're all a potential candidate for OCS all right, only we call it Officers Cooking School.

If you morons screw up in basic training, you're going to end up as an official Air Force cook for the officers. So unless you want to spend four years in the kitchen over a hot stove, you'd better shape up and not make me mad. Now get your butts on that bus."

Needless to say, I didn't go to any OCS; Officers Candidate School or the Officers Cooking School.

After basic training, I was transferred to Keesler Air Force Base in Biloxi, Mississippi, to learn how to send and receive Morse Code. In those days, the quickest and most secure way to send encrypted messages was with Morse Code. With a strong transmitter and a strong receiver, the signal could be sent or received pretty much around the world.

The United States Air Force Security Service had a ring of listening posts all around the world to intercept and decipher Russian military messages so we would always be aware of movements of their military and their aircraft. After finishing technical school at Keesler, I was assigned to a listening post on Shemya, a small island in the middle of the Bering Sea. It was the next-to-last island in the Aleutian Islands.

My Barracks on Shemya

The last island in the chain, Attu, could be seen from Shemya. Attu had been taken in a surprise attack by the Japanese army on June 7, 1942, exactly six months after Pearl Harbor. It was a part of Alaska, the only American incorporated territory taken by Japan during the war, and was occupied by Japanese troops for almost a year.

In the battle to retake Attu in May, 1943, 2,351 Japanese soldiers were killed as well as 549 Americans. The majority of the Japanese soldiers were killed in a kamikaze attack after their commander realized they were going to lose Attu to the Americans.

As I sat at my desk in the middle of the long dark Alaskan winter nights with the earphones on, typing the encoded Russian military messages sent in Morse Code, with the temperature outside at ten degrees below zero and the wind blowing at sixty miles per hour, whistling through the cracks in the old Quonset hut left over from World War II, I began to regret my decision not to accept the transfer by Kress's to Hempstead, Long Island, New York.

Knowing how to intercept Russian military coded messages was a wonderful skill, but I didn't believe there would be a great demand for it in the civilian world.

I was able to save $600 during my four years in the Air Force. I had taken out a military allotment for Mother when I enlisted in the Air Force. The allotment took approximately two-thirds of my military pay. My net pay each month was minimal. However, there was nothing to do on Shemya that cost money so being stationed there was a fortuitous event.

My younger brother, Gerald, had recently enlisted in the Air Force and he took his turn, after Jack, our older brother, and me, in providing a military allotment for our mother.

Six years after graduating from NHHS and four years after leaving S. H. Kress & Company, I was discharged in December, 1960, at McChord Air Force Base in Tacoma, Washington. I bought a Greyhound bus ticket and headed home with $600 in my bank account and dreams of a college degree in my hope account.

ABOUT THE AUTHOR

Kenan Maready was born and lived in Duplin County, North Carolina, until his family moved to Wilmington, North Carolina in 1951. He graduated from New Hanover High School in 1954. Not having any hope of attending college, he began working for S. H. Kress & Co., as a manager trainee.

In 1957, in lieu of accepting a transfer to a store on Long Island, he enlisted in the Air Force and was assigned to the United States Air Force Security Service. After one year of training, he served two years at Elmendorf Air Force Base near Anchorage and one year on the island of Shemya, the next to last island (Attu), in the Aleutian Islands, located in the middle of the Bering Sea.

After his discharge, he attended Wake Forest University with a major in accounting. He earned his BBA degree in thirty-three months by taking as many credit hours as the university would allow each semester as well as attending summer school. He also held a part-time job during that time. He graduated in May, 1964 and returned to Wilmington to work with a CPA firm where he was made Partner in 1969.

He married his wife, Millie Maultsby Maready, in 1967. They have two sons, Ken Maready and Forrest Maready, and two grandchildren.

He has been a member of the First Baptist Church in Wilmington for over 64 years where he has served in numerous leadership positions. He has been a member of the Wilmington Lions Club for over 40 years where he has served in numerous leadership positions.

This is his third attempt at writing a book. Some people say he should have learned his lesson about writing as described in Chapter 37 of this book: "I Discover I'm Not a Writer".

His purpose is to leave a document for future generations of his family so they will know how their ancestors lived during the "good old days".

Made in the USA
Middletown, DE
09 September 2016